THE
TEAMING
CHURCH

Praise for *The Teaming Church*

"The time is right for a book like this. *Read it* and you will find out how to build teams; *get your church to read it,* and you will build a teaming culture."

—Mark Batterson, Author of *The Circle Maker*

"Robert Crosby in *The Teaming Church* teaches us the essence of a team. This book is a must for pastors, church leaders, and church workers."

—Guillermo & Milagros Aguayo, Founder & Senior Pastor at "La Casa del Padre," Lima, Peru

"This is a fascinating read, full of quotes and wisdom about the crucial element of any ministry. We all need to build or belong to a team, and Bob Crosby's book will teach you how!"

—Joel Hunter, Pastor, Northland Church, Orlando

"Every pastor, leader, and teacher should read this book! Robert Crosby has grounded his understanding of leadership on the biblical foundation laid in the Trinity--the Divine Community. This inspiring book will inform the ministry and work of everyone engaged in the very heart of the gospel through faithful leadership in a faith community."

—Robert E. Cooley, President Emeritus, Gordon-Conwell Theological Seminary

"Robert Crosby roots his understanding of 'team' not in popular culture, but in a rich understanding of the Trinity as the basis for how a church's community can actually thrive. *The Teaming Church* provides a foundation for any church leader who longs to build a church culture that truly empowers God's people."

—Byron D. Klaus, President, Assemblies of God Theological Seminary

"Robert Crosby shows how your church can increase its effectiveness, by working with, not around, the people that God gives you. Packed with biblical insight and practical suggestions, *The Teaming Church* will energize your ministry. Give it to your team and read it together!"

—J. Kent Edwards, Professor of Preaching and Leadership, Talbot Seminary

THE
TEAMING
CHURCH
Ministry in the Age
of Collaboration

Robert C. Crosby

Abingdon Press
Nashville

The Teaming Church
Ministry in an Age of Collaboration

Copyright © 2012 by Abingdon Press

Library of Congress Cataloging-in-Publication Data
Crosby, Robert.
   The teaming church : ministry in the age of collaboration / Robert C. Crosby.
     p. cm.
   Includes bibliographical references (p.   ).
   ISBN 978-1-4267-5101-1 (book - pbk. / trade pbk. : alk. paper) 1. Christian leadership.
2. Church group work. I. Title.
   BV652.1.C745 2012
   253—dc23
                                                                        2012027513

Scripture quotations noted CEB are taken from the Common English Bible. Copyright © 2011 by the Common English Bible. All rights reserved. Used by permission. www.Com monEnglishBible.com.

Scripture marked NIV is taken from the Holy Bible, NEW INTERNATIONAL VERSION®. Copyright © 1973, 1978, 1984 by International Bible Society. All rights reserved throughout the world. Used by permission of International Bible Society.

Scripture marked NIrV taken from the Holy Bible, NEW INTERNATIONAL READER'S VERSION®. Copyright © 1973, 1978, 1984 by International Bible Society. All rights reserved throughout the world. Used by permission of International Bible Society.

Scripture quotations marked (ESV) are from The Holy Bible, English Standard Version®, copyright © 2001 by Crossway Bibles, a publishing ministry of Good News Publishers. Used by permission. All rights reserved.

Scripture quotations marked (NLT) are taken from the *Holy Bible,* New Living Translation, copyright © 1996. Used by permission of Tyndale House Publishers, Inc., Wheaton, Illinois 60189. All rights reserved.

Scripture quotations marked *THE MESSAGE* are from *THE MESSAGE.* Copyright © by Eugene H. Peterson 1993, 1994, 1995, 1996, 2000, 2001, 2002. Used by permission of NavPress Publishing Group.

Scripture quotations marked NASB are taken from the *New American Standard Bible®*, Copyright © 1960, 1962, 1963, 1968, 1971, 1972, 1973, 1975, 1977, 1995 by The Lockman Foundation. Used by permission. (www.Lockman.org)

Scripture quotations marked *GOD'S WORD* are from *God's Word. God's Word* is a copyrighted work of God's Word to the Nations. Quotations are used by permission. Copyright 1995 by God's Word to the Nations. All rights reserved.

Scripture quotations marked ASV are from the American Standard Version of the Bible.

Scripture marked KJV is from the King James or Authorized Version of the Bible.

12 13 14 15 16 17 18 19 20 21—10 9 8 7 6 5 4 3 2 1

MANUFACTURED IN THE UNITED STATES OF AMERICA

READ Other Books and Resources by Robert Crosby
Living Life from the Soul
Conversation Starters for Couples
Conversation Starters for Parents and Kids
More Than a Savior: When Jesus Calls You Friend

READ Robert's Column—"Catch the Current"—at Patheos.com:
http://www.patheos.com/About-Patheos/Robert-Crosby.html

READ Robert's Blog "The Current"—also at Patheos.com:
http://www.patheos.com/blogs/robertcrosby/

DOWNLOAD mobile apps designed by Robert Crosby
to enrich your team, family, or marriage.
More information about the app and how to download it at:
http://www.globible.com/AskUp

"Follow my example, just like I follow Christ's." (1 Cor 11:1 CEB)

Facebook: http://www.facebook.com/robert.crosby.902
Twitter: @rccrosby

To

Rev. David H. Krist

For your prayers, your mentoring,
and for leading all your "teams" so well!

We are to tend to the depth of our relationships;
God will determine the breadth of our influence.
—Robert Crosby

How good and pleasant it is
    when brothers live together in unity! . . .
For there the LORD bestows his blessing,
    even life forevermore.
—Ps 133:1, 3b NIV

CONTENTS

Contents

FOREWORD

Prayer renews our passion for God, but teams put that passion to work. As surely as Jesus went from one place of prayer to another, in between he spent his time forming, teaching, and empowering his team, the Twelve. Christ-followers and churches today wanting to make an impact that exceeds and outlives them will spend much of their time building and working with their team. *The Teaming Church* is one of the best tools I have found on this vital subject of doing ministry in "the age of collaboration."

The time is right for a book like this. I believe you will connect with the effective and vivid way Bob describes the "teaming church" and the "teaming leader." These concepts and insights are profoundly biblical but have a clarity that is easy to get your head around. Also, I noticed something else that really captured my attention: the principles and insights go deeper as you read further. *Read this book* and you will find out how to build teams; *get your church to read it*, and you will build a teaming culture. My favorite chapter is actually the last one because it paints such a clear picture of the difference between strong teams and weak ones. You will want to visit and revisit that chapter with your team. I plan to.

Make no mistake, however. Building strong teams is no easy task; it requires insight and intentionality. I'm excited to see how God will use this resource to help equip and encourage pastors, leaders, and churches. While my most recent book, *The Circle Maker*, focused on helping people draw circles of prayer in and around their communities, this book focuses on helping you draw another kind of circle. Bob calls them "circles of honor" and makes a strong case for how teaming circles reflect the ultimate "team," the Trinity. That insight alone adds significance and weight to the important work of building church teams. As it turns out teams not only help us do the work of God, they also can actually reflect the glory of God. Now that's exciting!

The Teaming Church contends that the time in which we live requires one ministry skill perhaps more than any other: collaboration. The description of the vital role collaboration plays, and will play, in our churches and communities is spot on. While growth-driven leaders focus on putting people to work, teaming leaders aim at getting people to work *together*.

There is a difference; one that moves us from doing the work of the church our way to doing it God's way, the teaming way.

I urge you to read this book, get your leaders reading it, and, if you're really serious about teams, get your whole church to read it and work through it together. It will help put you, your teams, and your church on the same page and keep you there. And, that's a good place to be.

Start drawing circles everywhere and expect great things to happen through your team!

Mark Batterson
Lead Pastor
National Community Church
Washington, DC
www.theaterchurch.com

ACKNOWLEDGMENTS

The Teaming Church was a team project. You would have to be crazy to write a book about teams and teaming leadership all alone.

I could not have completed this book without an incredible home team. My wife, Pamela, has been patient and understanding with my writing schedule to the point of long-suffering. Sweetheart, the suffering is over and I'm taking you out!

I have led churches, church ministries, citywide outreach teams, a university student body, and a youth group, but my favorite team to lead is my kids—Kristin, Kara, Rob, and Kandace. When it comes to temperament surveys, I think all of you score differently. It seems we have one of each of the four main types, which keeps our family lively, hopping, fun, and never without an opinion. Variety is the spice of life, of families and of teams.

My parents—Bob and Beverly Crosby—led the first "team" I ever became a part of, a team of four: two parents, my brother Ned, who is also a pastor, and me. You both always made us feel like we were your first and most important team. Thank you for that! And, thank you to my wife's parents, Dave and Shirley Krist, who made room for me in their family circle too.

After years of pastoring and leading teams, I now have a pastor of my own for the first time in my adult life. Jeff Sellers, thank you for your friendship, for opening your trusted pulpit to me, and for all those great team talks at Starbucks. I am blessed to call you my pastor.

Thank you to everyone who consented to let me interview you on this subject and those of you who looked over the early versions of the manuscript. Thanks to Tommy Barnett, Wayne Blackburn, Jason Burns, Del Chittim, Robert E. Cooley, Rod Cooper, Kent Edwards, Bobby Gruenewald, Craig Groeschel, Sam Hemby, Joel Hunter, Kent Ingle, Rod Loy, Joe Lyons, Murphy Matheny, Dan McBride, Ed Plastow, Samuel Rodriguez, Jeff Sellers, and Terry Storch.

From the meal at Red Lobster that Pam and I had with Blythe Daniel less than a year ago, we knew that our prayer for an enthusiastic literary agent had been answered big time! Thanks for being so encouraging about this project and others yet to come.

I appreciate Paul Franklin, Kathy Armistead, Connie Stella, Hampton Ryan, and their publishing team at Abingdon Press and am excited about this first book together.

Of course, a huge source of my inspiration is the students of Southeastern University in Lakeland, Florida. Your eager interest to learn, your challenging questions, and your passion for Christ and his presence never cease to amaze me. I am blessed and privileged to serve you. I love what God is doing in and through your generation!

To those who have agreed to pray with me about this project—you know who you are, you know what I've asked, and we will see what God does!

Finally, to all of the pastors around the world—you are my heroes. I have served for many years as one of you and I know the joys and challenges of that vital role. I pray every day for you, I stand with you, and I have asked God that this resource would be one of the ways he allows me to help hold up your arms as Aaron and Hur did for Moses (Exod 17:9-13).

This book has been written especially for pastors, church leaders, and church workers. It is designed to be used as a training tool for pastors and church leaders to use with their teams, team leaders, team members, and workers in the church of all kinds.

The design of *The Teaming Church* lends itself well to use right within your ministry team, for training, for encouragement, for reflection, and for evaluation. Each chapter has a few questions at the end to further your conversations about the insights and material.

If you are a pastor, I would encourage you to read through the book and then consider equipping your congregation and leadership by getting all of your teams on the same page about teaming ministry.

If you are a worker in a church, I suggest you read the book and, if it strikes a chord, pass it on to your pastor. Let your pastor know that as you read it you thought that he or she may find it helpful and encouraging.

Ultimately, my hope and prayer for this book is that it will be a part of an answer to a prayer that Jesus actually prayed: "I pray they will be one, Father, just as you are in me and I am in you" (John 17:21 CEB). May it strengthen pastors, help equip churches, and build unity in the body of Christ.

Once Upon a Team—A Story

A Cup of Coffee and a Much-Needed Mentor
7:28 A.M.
a Thursday
the local café

Scott Sanders had a problem, and the one thing he needed most was quickly running out—time. Leaning back in his chair at the café down the street from his church, the young pastor moved his eyes away from the online version of *USA Today*, took a sip of his morning brew, and let out another sigh, the fourth such sigh since he had arrived.

The café door swung open and in walked Scott's appointment, Glenn Anderson. Glenn had served as a senior pastor for twenty-nine years at New Hope Church, about fifteen minutes away from Scott's church. Now semi-retired, Glenn served at the same church as care pastor.

Feeling the need for a mentor, Scott had asked for the meeting. The challenges of working with a diverse group of people and the temptations of life in general had moved this need up on his priority list. He had made a few attempts at garnering a spiritual father of sorts years earlier, but to date all such efforts had failed. He hoped that a growing friendship might emerge from this effort and figured it was at least worth one more try.

"Hey, Pastor Glenn, how are you this morning?" Scott asked.

"Hi, Scott," Glenn said. "Good to see you, young man."

Young was about the last thing Scott was feeling at the moment.

5

"Good to see you too," Scott said, "and thanks for meeting with me, Pastor."

"Hey, let's drop the prefixes, okay? Just call me Glenn, please."

"It works for me."

After a few minutes of ordering coffees, munching on doughnuts, and covering some of the most recent news in sports, politics, and the church, Glenn asked the right question: "So, tell me. What is the big challenge you are facing this week?"

Encouraged by the concern, Scott smiled, sat up straight in his seat, and took a deep breath. "Well. Can I be really honest with you? I mean, really honest?"

"Anything else would be a disappointment, and probably a bit boring."

Scott laughed and then leaned forward. "Ahhh. Alright, then, where do I start?" He raised his eyes momentarily to the ceiling and back down.

"Start with the one you are *most* concerned about today," Glenn said.

"Okay. That's easy. It's a problem with one of my team members; my worship leader."

"You mean the one who led worship at our sectional ministers' event last month?"

"The same."

"Well. That boy can sure sing! He is one talented young man."

"Talented, yes," Scott said, shaking his head. "Wise, not so much."

"What is his name again?"

"Tyler."

"Unwise? How so? What's going on with this young man?"

"Well, as much as I appreciate his work ethic and musical skills, there is something missing. I mean, there is no doubt that he has improved the quality of music in our services, but the more I work with this guy, the more apparent it becomes that too often his number one priority is simply himself, not the team."

"What has he done to make you come to this conclusion?"

"It's his attitude. It has shown up in some periodic explosions in staff meetings, rehearsals, and even one budget committee meeting."

"Really?"

"Yes. Board members noticed it and now most of our worship team members are really frustrated. So much so, another one just came to meet with me after their rehearsal to say it would be their last night."

"What was their concern, specifically?"

"Apparently Tyler lost it when he was giving instructions to the group. It was over something simple like how they were going to harmonize on a chorus or something like that. The rehearsal started to unravel when, unsolicited, a few of the band members started offering suggestions. Tyler obviously did not want any suggestions and was getting more upset with every comment, until finally, he just lost it."

"Scott, you have used that phrase a couple of times, 'lost it.' How?"

"When people started offering advice, Tyler just started yelling, 'Stop it! Every one of you just shut up! I don't recall asking any of you for advice.' One vocalist commented, 'But, we were just offering a couple of suggestions.' That lit his fuse. I'm told that Tyler let it all go and said, 'No. I don't want your suggestions. I don't want any of them. Don't you understand? I am the leader and you are just members of the team. Now just keep your opinions to yourself, sing your part the way I told you and just let me lead this team! I'm the leader; you're not. Understand?' That's why they all ended up in my office."

"My goodness, that must have been awkward," Glenn said.

"Oh, yeah, knowing this guy, terribly so. But I feel responsible. I hired him. It would not surprise me if most of the worship team just ends up resigning. I'm really stuck on this one and don't have a clue about what to do next. So, now you know what my biggest challenge today is. That's it! Any suggestions?"

"Scott, let me ask you a couple of other questions."

"Shoot."

"For one, how would you describe the spirit in which these disgruntled team members came to you? Were they upset, angry?"

"Actually, they were really more sad than mad. I don't think any of them could be described as angry. Actually, I'm the one feeling angry about this. I am really ticked at this guy for treating the people I pastor this way."

"So, if they aren't angry, what is their issue?"

"I believe they are 'hurt,' hurt by leadership."

"Hmmmm."

"Hurt and disappointed."

"So, my next question. What are you going to do about it?" Glenn inquired.

"Ha. That's what I was hoping you were going to be able to tell me!" Scott said.

"Well, I'm not sure I can, or even should, 'tell' you what to do, but we certainly can explore your options together. How about that?"

"I would really appreciate it," Scott said. He leaned forward on the table, feeling reassured by the tone of experience he heard in Glenn's voice and eager to resolve the problem.

"Scott, as a leader, what are your values?"

"What do you mean by 'values'? My moral values?"

"I mean your values when it comes to people. Let me ask it this way. What is it that you value about people that Tyler violated at this particular rehearsal?"

"Well, respect, for one."

"Explain what you mean by 'respect.'"

"I don't care who you are or what your title is, pastor, worship pastor, deacon, elder, or even the president of the United States; no title or position ever gives you the right to talk down to people. We are supposed to treat people, all people, with respect and dignity."

"Where did you develop this value?"

"Oh, my dad and mom drilled that one into me, for one. But, honestly, it really became more of a deep-seated conviction during my college years when I served at a homeless shelter. I became so aware when I saw that every person has a soul and that a soul is a priceless gift of God."

Glenn leaned forward a bit and said, "You learned something valuable that summer, Scott, something that shapes who you are today. But, do you think your worship leader has learned it?"

"Obviously not."

"So, then, why did you hire him in the first place?"

"That's a good question."

"Something motivated you to hire him."

"Well, first of all, his resume looked great. He really turned on the charm during the interview process and impressed our board and, like you said, the boy can sing."

"But," Glenn continued, "I gather that you feel he is missing the important value you would refer to as. . . ." Glenn paused for Scott to fill in the blank.

"Respect," Scott said.

"You could call it that, I suppose. But, I think I have a better word for it. A biblical word, in fact."

"You do? What's that? What word?"

"I tell you what, Scott. After we get a warm up on our coffees, then I'll tell you."

"Sounds like a plan."

The Circles Jesus Drew

Have you ever found yourself in a circle of honor? I did for just a few minutes several years ago. They were life-transforming minutes and I will never be the same.

What happened in that circle is something I never expected. Sure, I might have hoped to be honored a bit at my sixteenth birthday party (or perhaps my sixtieth someday), at my high school graduation party, wedding reception, or some other more expected place of honoring, but not here, and not in such a public place. It caught me by surprise.

For me, the circle of honor came in an old church hallway in downtown Columbia, South Carolina, just moments before my water baptism. Barely seventeen years old and newly converted to Christ, I was in the foyer of my downtown home church wearing a robe and making my way toward the baptistry when it happened. My then sixty-eight year old pastor, standing in line next to my unsuspecting parents and me, enthusiastically asked a visiting guest speaker, "Have you met this young man? (*looking toward me*) Well, let me introduce you to him. This is Robert Crosby. (*Is he talking about me?* I wondered.) God is doing great things in this young man's life and we are excited about his future!"

The circle of honor I found myself in on the night I was water baptized only lasted about one minute at the most, but the effects of it have lasted a lifetime and, in some ways, are still with me to this day. Although my pastor had ministerial duties to perform that night such as baptizing a bunch of new believers, hosting a guest evangelist, and leading the congregation, and no more than a few moments to spare, the words he chose filled something within me. At once I felt affirmed, appreciated, and, yes, significant. I felt *honored*. In less than than two minutes, someone I greatly looked up to, fifty years older than I, had created a circle of honor around me.

A Teaming Approach

Pastors and church leaders need effective and relevant ways to involve people in ministry amid today's fast-paced, changing world. Sometimes, however, it can be challenging to know where to begin, or how.

In a world where leaders had drawn triangles and hierarchies, Jesus came on the scene drawing circles: circles of honor, circles of teamwork, and circles of community. These circles were nurtured by a culture of authentic honor that his followers found irresistible and ultimately reproducible. Jesus' practice showed that the most effective biblical strategy to assist pastors in building churches is to draw what I like to call circles of honor, or to employ a teaming approach.

The thing that sets a ministry team apart from all others is that when it is led in a truly biblical fashion, it becomes a circle of honor. A biblical team is not just a group of people pulled together to get a job done; it is something more. While most teams in churches today are set up to be *working* teams, a ministry team is more, much more. It is an environment in which a person is able to thrive, emerge in their giftedness, and reflect the glory of God.

A Forgotten Word

In many minds, the word *honor* evokes thoughts of kings, brave knights, damsels in distress, and chivalry. Some associate honor with Asian cultures that show respect for their elders and one another. The word reminds some of the military, and the Marines in particular, with their famed code of honor. While honor still exists in certain pockets of our society, for the most part it has gone AWOL, replaced with cheap substitutes such as self-actualization, self-talk, and self-esteem.

How does the Bible define honor?

In the Old Testament, most occurrences of honor are some form of the Hebrew word *kabod*, which means "heavy" or "weighty." It is a word also translated as "glory." It suggests the magnitude or greatness of someone or something such as the "glory" of God. In the New Testament, the Greek word for honor means to value highly, to esteem, and to not take lightly.

The idea of honor in the Bible is deeply relational. It reflects how people in a society, group, community, or team relate to God and to one another. It is the glue of true community, the right stuff of true teams. The Bible not only teaches the importance of honor, it also gives us what could arguably be referred to as "The 10 Principles of Honor." A closer look at the

Ten Commandments reveals that each one has to do with one of two things: honoring God and honoring our fellow men and women.

The Honor Deficit

An honoring culture flows with regular praise and recognition. It is characterized by consistent mutual support and affirmations.

In *The Carrot Principle*, Adrian Gostick and Chester Elton cite that 69 percent of North American workers reported that they were not recognized at all in their jobs last year. And, if that is not alarming enough, 79 percent of the top performers who change jobs reported that one of the main reasons was a lack of recognition for the work they had done. Perhaps most amazing in the research was the discovery that organizations that effectively recognize and praise their employees are three times as profitable as those who do not.

Not only are we living today in a culture that is losing its way in affirming and honoring people, it has at the same time become more adept at sarcasm and criticism. In such a world, circles of honor stand out and "shine like stars in the world" (Phil 2:15 CEB). Circles of honor are rare and much needed finds.

In her book, *Teaming: How Organizations Learn, Innovate and Compete in the Knowledge Economy*, Amy Edmondson says: "Today, people engaging in teaming at work need to be responsible, accountable individuals who respect [that is, honor] each other, understand the inevitability of conflict, and accept the responsibility to sort through such difficulties." Edmondson, a Harvard professor and leadership researcher, acknowledges the vital role of respect (that is, honor) on teams.

The Honoring Circle

The Trinity is the ultimate example of honor. For as long as I can remember, I have believed in the doctrine of the Trinity, but I did not know how it related to me or to the church, for that matter, until more recently. For years in my mind, the Trinity was a concept far too transcendent and complex to ever grasp. Theologically speaking, it is the core of Christian doctrine—that one God simultaneously exists in one substance and in three persons, the Father, Son, and Holy Spirit. God is one, revealed in three distinct forms. The Trinity may be the single most important model for all human relationships and teams—a model of honoring. The Trinity is, in fact, the original circle of honor—the Divine Team. A closer look at how the three forms of the Trinity interact with one another affirms this truth. The Trinity is a perfect circle of honor: a true teaming environment, the ultimate One. The Father, the Son, and the Spirit constantly reflect honor upon one another. Great teams, as well, strive to do the same. There is neither a better model nor example than this for groups and teams within the church today.

Teams and Community

As churches endeavor to find more effective and fulfilling ways to engage people in ministry, the team approach fits the renewed clamoring for community within churches today. Such an approach seems more conducive to experiencing church as an organism as opposed to an organization. Gilbert Bilezikian describes it this way:

> In our day, there is a clamor for the church to rediscover its identity as community. Many Christian leaders bemoan the fact that the church has lost its basic biblical definition as [a] divinely designed community. Lay people and clergy alike express dissatisfaction with churches conducting their business as if it were a business. They compare the stilted and stultifying routines of their church life to the effervescent explosion of Holy-Spirit-generated vitality that enabled the church of Pentecost to conquer the ancient world for Christ. . . . They demand a radical return to the basics of biblical teachings about the church as community.[1]

While the Holy Spirit was the source of the early church's effectiveness, teams and teaming efforts were arguably the strategy from the disciples of Christ to the missionary journeys of Paul and beyond. The circles of community and honor within the church provide a place for people to be "built up" spiritually, emotionally, and relationally; as a result, the church is built up. One pastor of several decades came to this conclusion about the role of a pastor: "None of us are called to our success, but to the success of our people. We are not called to build big churches, but to build big people."

Jesus Drew Circles

One of the worst mistakes a team leader can make is to allow his or her team to feel undervalued. A key part of a team leader's or facilitator's role is to remind the team of how valuable and important they are to one another, to the church, to the leadership and, most of all, to God himself and to his high purposes on earth.

> What is man that you are mindful of him,
> and the son of man that you care for him?
> You . . . crowned him with glory and honor. (Ps 8:4-5 ESV)

Jesus drew circles. He drew circles of honor and called people into them. He built teams and communities in ways that people found absolutely compelling and frequently irresistible. He honored others everywhere he went. During his earthly ministry he constantly crowned people with honor, particularly and uniquely those who had been dishonored and disenfranchised by the world around them. Think of all the "crowns" he placed on unsuspecting heads, including the woman at the well, the ten lepers, a bunch of fishermen, tax collectors, a woman caught in the act of adultery, little children, and even a widow who barely had two pennies to rub together. To each of them, he gave a crown of honor.

Christ was the ultimate teaming leader.

When Jesus left heaven and came to earth, he stepped beyond the Trinity's circle of honor in which he dwelt and he drew a new one: a new circle. The first circle of honor he formed included all those who followed Him, especially his twelve disciples. He drew them into a tight team, this fellowship of honor and community, only to send them out to draw other circles of their own, communities of faith, vibrant teams, as well. On one occasion, Jesus prayed to the Father about these other circles he had drawn:

> [My prayer is that they] are one: I in them and you in me.
> May they be brought to complete unity to let the world know
> that you sent me and have loved them even as you have loved
> me." (John 17:22-23 NIV)

There is dramatic tension as Jesus intercedes between the two great circles in which God, the Father, allowed him to be a part. He looks at one circle in light of another. He asks that the circle of disciples be brought into a relational unity that reflects the same experience he had in the Divine Circle, the Trinity. Here's what he prayed: "that they may be one as we are one: I in them and you in me" (John 17:22-23 NIV).

The Teaming Church Principle #1—
An Honoring Community

I have been working in and on teams, building, shaping, and studying them, for more than twenty-five years. Throughout my journey it has become unmistakably clear that there are four primary characteristics of an effective church or ministry team. I have listed them in a brief statement that I call "The Teaming Church Principle":

> To become a great team your group must have a deeply challenging goal, a creatively empowering leader, and a collaborative, biblically honoring community.

This statement is made up of four key components, all of which are vital to the success of a team:

- **The Character** represents *the right kind of people and practices* on the team. They must be honorable and treat one another with honor.

- **The Carrot** represents *the right kind of challenge* the team faces or is called to take on. It must be bigger than any one individual and absolutely compelling.

- **The Coach** represents *the right kind of leader* the team needs in order to thrive—a true teaming leader.

- **The Community** represents *the right kind of culture* in which teams can continue to grow and develop—a teaming context.

While the final three characteristics of a great team are specifically named, the first is embedded in the final description: "biblically honoring." In a sense, we will start with the end in mind.

> To become a great team your group must have a deeply challenging goal, a creatively empowering leader, and a collaborative, *biblically honoring* community.

Honor represents the character of a great team. It is one of the things that makes a great team great. An authentically biblical team is perhaps best described not only as a circle, but also as an *honoring* circle. Honor permeates the atmosphere of a truly biblical team. It sets it apart and produces something not only productive and practical, but also something glorious. In a marvelous and mysterious sense, it replicates a sense of the glory that is the Trinity.

Drawing Circles

Every person in the world needs a circle of honor in which to dwell, live, and thrive. God has designed us that way. By our very nature, we just do not do well on our own ("It is not good that the man should be alone"—Gen 2:18 NRSV). We are made to thrive in communities and on true teams. We are not just called to live, but to do life together. We are not just called to worship, but to worship together. We are not just called to serve, but to serve together. The church itself is intended to be a circle of honor—a network of relationships in which we honor God and one another.

You might say we are never more like God than when we are drawing circles. The Bible commands us to do so ("Honor everyone"—1 Pet 2:17a NRSV). When we honor the people around us and welcome them into the fellowship of that honor, when we work this way on teams and small groups, we are doing something God has always done and is always doing—drawing circles. We are answering Jesus' John 17 prayer and reflecting the Trinity itself.

Fatal Teaming Error #1

One common mistake that diminishes a team and its potential is undervaluing the team. A lack of honor from the team leader or facilitator demotivates and discourages the soul of a team. There are perhaps few things more frustrating than being on a team where the leader does not affirm and appreciate the work and the varied contributions of the team and the team members.

When you draw a circle of honor around someone, something powerful happens. In a culture quick to dishonor, you refresh a soul by seeing him or her the way God does—as someone made to reflect his image. When you draw a circle of honor around someone, you create a sneak preview of heaven and reflect something ultimately found in one place—the original Circle of Honor, the Divine Team, the Trinity—just by drawing a circle.

The Trinity, then, is not some stilted and saintly group of celestial beings. On the contrary, the Trinity is a vibrant, divine team of fully engaged Persons, engaged with one another and with creation. But, what will it take to get our ministry groups, committees, and churches to function in a similar manner? What will it take to turn the group into a true team?

Drawing Your Circle

Questions to Ask Your Team

1. Have you ever found yourself in a circle of honor? When and where? What was the experience like?

17

2. Do you think there is a honor deficit in our culture today? In the church? How so?

3. In what way is the Trinity an honoring circle?

4. What were some of the circles of honor Jesus drew?

5. Where are some of the places you believe God wants you to draw circles of honor?

6. What are some things that make people feel truly honored?

Part One

Draw Your Circle
Creating a Team

Building a great team as a ministry leader involves knowing how to draw circles in which people can come together, worship together, serve together, and thrive!

Once Upon a Team—Scene Two

The Second Cup

Glenn poured a packet of raw sugar into his cup and started stirring. "So you want to know my word for it?"

"I do," Scott said.

"Well, let me warn you, it is a word that has gotten a bit dusty. Some would say it is antiquated, but I think it is overdue for a reintroduction."

"And, what is it?" Scott was eager.

"What do you think?"

"Hmmm, a synonym for 'respect'? Oh, I don't know . . . umm . . . esteem, admiration, dignity?"

"Well, those are words, but not the one I'm looking for."

"Okay, I give up. What is it?"

"Honor."

"Oh, yeah, I have to admit; I haven't heard that one much lately, except maybe in an ad for the marines."

"Hah. That's right! My dad was a marine, and he drilled it into our minds as kids—the three marine values."

"A drill sergeant, huh?"

"No. He was actually pretty mild mannered, but, man oh man, he was sold on those three values."

"Which are . . . ?"

"Sure. Honor, courage, and commitment."

"Sounds like a great basic training for some Christians, huh?"

"Well, Scott, I'm sure you know quite well that before the marines ever chose to use it, *honor* was a biblical word. It shows up more than two hundred times in the NIV Bible."

"You must have preached a sermon on this recently or something."

"Oh, I've preached dozens on the subject over the years. I actually designed a series of messages at one point on honor. More, of late, I've discovered a need to talk about it one-on-one, like today with you."

"That's a good thing," Scott said, nodding.

"I think it is. And, I also think that you, Scott, are a person of honor. I can tell. Honor means something to you. Respect is a good thing; but honor is a great thing."

"It's sort of tough to define, though, isn't it?"

"I suppose you're right," Glenn said. "Tough to define, but you sure know when someone is conveying honor and you know when they aren't, don't you?"

"Oh, yes. That's for certain. I wish my worship leader was sitting here right now to hear this."

"It is probably something that is more modeled than even defined or dissected; better caught, than taught, as they say."

"So true. What the worship leader did to his team that night at practice was the opposite of honoring them or their God-given abilities."

"That's right. It was dishonoring, disruptive, and even destructive. And, remember, the same thing that can tear a soul apart is what can also tear a team apart."

"A lack of honor?" Scott asked.

"Yes. In a word—dishonor; it's a team killer. I believe dishonor has hurt so many lives, families, and churches over the years."

"So do you think that's the real problem I am facing with this guy, just a lack of respect?"

"No. It is not just 'a lack of respect' but of failing to affirm and honor the people on the team," Glenn said. "Church and business leaders alike have a God-given responsibility to build up the person in order to build up the organization. The church will only feel as affirmed and strong as her people do."

"So, then, dishonor is deadly?"

"Like I said before, it's a team killer. One of the top three, I would say."

"What are the other two?"

"Oh, those are for another day. But, don't worry, we'll get to them, alright, but one at a time. For now, back to my earlier question. "So, what are you going to do about it?'"

"I was afraid you might ask that one again. I'm not sure. A part of me wants to call Tyler into my office when I get there this morning and just ream him out. Another part wants to sever the relationship, to let him go; to just fire him. Honestly, I think that would make some people really happy, but there would be others who may leave the church over it."

"I know it is a tight spot to be in. I've been there myself."

"And, honestly, his attitude is not the only one I am dealing with. Since I took over as senior pastor at the church two years ago, it seems that rotten attitudes have popped up in more than a few places."

"And, how have you dealt with those problems or problem people?"

"I just keep putting fires out everywhere I can. I just try to choose my battles, overlook what I can, and confront people when I absolutely have to."

"How's that working out for you?"

"Well, I did call you to meet for coffee this morning, didn't I?"

Smiling a knowing smile, Glenn said, "Ha. Yes, you did. Well, then, let's zoom the lens out a bit farther for a minute, shall we? How would you say the church is doing in general? What are you feeling? What are you sensing? I mean, is it growing? Vibrant? Connected? United? Disconnected? What is the overall mood or spirit that you sense?"

"Stuck."

"You feel stuck?"

"The whole church feels stuck."

"Organizationally 'stuck'?"

"Shoot, not only that, we even feel emotionally stuck, financially stuck, spiritually stuck, and growth stuck. It feels like we are in a bit of a rut, you know, sluggish and predictable."

"You say 'emotionally stuck.' That's interesting. Is that how you would describe the worship team right now?"

"Absolutely; it is probably the worst team at the church. Actually, my vision is that it would be a truly worshipful and united group, but ironically it is probably the most divided and competitive one in the whole church right now."

"So," Glenn asked, "if the worship team is the worst team, which one is the best?"

"The best team? I don't think any of our groups are functioning as true teams, not the kind you have just described, except . . ."

"Except what?"

"There is one pretty incredible group in the church, but they are not really an official group like a board, committee, or governing group."

"Who are they?"

"Our senior adult small group."

"Really? Why is that?"

"Because they are the most united, selfless, humble, consistent, and come to think of it, honoring group of people I can think of."

"Honoring? Now, there's an interesting word," Glenn said, smiling. "How so?"

Scott slid his chair back and stood up. "After we get another warm up on our coffees, and maybe another doughnut, I'll tell you."

"I think I heard that somewhere before."

Chapter One

The Day Your Group Becomes a Team

*The purpose of a team is to make the strengths of each person
effective and his or her weaknesses irrelevant.*
—Peter Drucker

Something happens when a group turns into a team. Something not
always easy to put into words, but undeniable and unmistakable once experienced. When a group becomes supercharged with a compelling challenge,
opportunity, or even an obstacle, for that matter, team spirit can take over
in amazing ways.

Americans moved from a *group* of people into a *forming team* the
moment George W. Bush borrowed the firefighter's bullhorn at Ground
Zero and rallied a nation to action together following the tragic events
of 9/11. In that moment, regardless of political persuasion, Americans
recognized that the country had been brutally attacked. A need was
deeply felt. Amidst that need a leader's voice pierced the silence and
read the mood of the masses, bringing a sudden sense of urgency and
clarity, of resolve and focus. As a result, a teaming spirit emerged in
the souls of Americans. Immediately, and for a time, differences melted
away and a common cause forged into a new sense of community, resolve, and teamwork. America became focused; no longer a nation divided, now a team with a mission. If only for a while, the combination
of a shared challenge and a shared resolve, understood and called out by
a team leader, helped to turn a group in to a team.

In forming great teams, one key ingredient is present: a goal. Not
just any goal, but a compelling and clear goal. I like to think of it as the

team's "carrot." The carrot is the clear, enticing, and compelling goal, the so-wonderful-you-can-almost-taste-it goal that is set out before all of the team members.

When we move from just a *group* of people and become a team, our smaller, personal visions and dreams are overtaken by great, corporate goals and a common mission. Sometimes this transformation can start to happen in an unexpected moment of crisis. In these cases the challenges and goals can quickly and suddenly become quite clear and compelling. More challenging is the intentional process of turning a group into a team within organizations who are perhaps not in an immediate crisis but simply groups of people in need of vision, focus, and direction.

Changing Times—Changing Skills

group [groop]	(*noun*) Any collection or assemblage of persons.
team [teem]	(*noun*) A group of people associated in some joint action.

One reason teaming churches and teaming leaders are so needed today is because our world is so rapidly changing—arguably more than at any other time in history. In North America, for example, history thus far could arguably be divided into four periods:

The Agricultural Age (1776–1889)

The Industrial Age (1890–1989)

The Informational Age (1990–2010)

The Present Age? (2011–??)

In order to thrive in The Agricultural Age, you had to know how to cultivate. To succeed or even to get by in life, most people had to play a part in growing some kind of produce or livestock.

Success in The Industrial Age involved knowing how to create or sell a product. As factories and industries emerged, numerous products were invented and mass-produced.

In The Informational Age, however, tables have changed significantly. Information itself, long held in the private and controlling grasp of proletariats, has now become the chief commodity. New, better, and faster means of technology have emerged to make information more engaging and accessible. Because of this the essential skill has been communication.

But now, it appears that we are moving into yet another age of history. This time, however, globalism has increased the effect. Much of the world is experiencing this change. We are moving out of one age and into another. Can you sense it?

We now live in a new flatter world. At a time when we are not just connected by technology, we are hyperconnected by social networks. As some have suggested, you could call it The Imaginational Age. This new period is significantly changing the systems by which we live, work, and share information, and in some ways is creating entirely new systems. It will require us to use parts of our brains that perhaps have been otherwise disengaged. It will call for new depths of imagination.

Now before you accuse me of getting all Disney on you with the word "imaginational," hear me out. We now live in an age and environment of such rapid change and opportunity that no one mind and no sole person can effectively and independently navigate the challenges and the opportunities we face. It now takes a team, a collaborative blending of ideas, intuition, and inspirations. Our world, and the opportunities and problems we face, have become increasingly complex. They require teaming efforts, ideas, and strategies as never before. In yesterday's world you could have gotten along by your ability to cultivate, create, or communicate. Many did, but no longer. In order to succeed in The Imaginational Age there is a new essential skill you will need. With it, you and your church will be at a significant advantage. Without it, you will be limited. The new essential is that you will have to know how to collaborate.

Collaborate

The time for teams and teaming in leadership is not coming—it is here. It has arrived. The question is, have you? People in churches, businesses, and other organizations are no longer responding the way they used to toward hierarchical maneuverings and manipulations. They are tired of being pushed; they instead want to be drawn and inspired with the sense that they are a part of something greater than themselves, that they have a share in building the kingdom of God.

The Defined Team

Teams have existed in various forms and manners throughout history. Trey Thoelcke said it well:

> People have always worked in collaborative units—either for the ca-maraderie and social interactions with others, or for the benefits of their diverse points of view, support, and skills. There have always been tasks too great for one person to tackle alone, such as early tribes hunting large animals, or tasks that require people with different skills and talents to compete, such as playing a Mozart symphony, building a space capsule, or constructing a modern house. Teams are a fundamental unit of organizing people to meet new challenges and achieve results.[1]

Here are a few terms we need to define:

team—After considering several alternatives, I developed the following definition for the purposes of this book: a ministry team is a small number of Christ-followers with complementary skills who are committed to common purposes, performance goals, and approaches for which they hold themselves mutually accountable.[2]

teambuilding—This term represents equipping Christians into ministry teams. This incorporates effective collaboration between Christian workers, both paid staff and volunteers, and involves clear communication, empowerment, mutual accountability, trust, and selflessness.

teaming—This term, contained in the title, is both a verb and an adjective. As a verb, teaming describes efforts made to work as a team or team player. For example, a group of volunteers "teaming toward their goal" is endeavoring to do so in an intentional, collaborative manner, as opposed to an independent approach. Additionally, the term is used as an adjective to describe an individual or organization committed to a teambuilding approach. Thus, the "teaming church" is a church focused on accomplishing its mission and work by incorporating people into teams rather than through groups of individuals. Also, the "teaming pastor" or "teaming deacon" is one who is committed to accomplishing ministry in a collaborative, rather than individualistic, manner.

Great Goals Equal Great Teams

You cannot have a great team without a great goal. It is simply impossible. As Christian leaders and pastors we sometimes think that if we simply bring a group of believers together and talk about being a great team, we will automatically become one. It is not so. My recommendation is, don't try it. Merely calling a group your team will not turn it into one. Don't just call your group a team; treat them like a team. Don't just teach about honor; practice it. To become a great team, you must have great love for your team members, but you also must have a great goal and effectively hold that goal over the team, encouraging and challenging them toward it.

The Teaming Church Principle #2: A Deeply Challenging Goal

Great goals are the motivators that draw on our God-given desires and potentials. This is true for individuals, but more so for a team. The goal or the carrot is the motivation of a great team. It is the second teaming essential: to become a great team your group must have *a deeply challenging goal*, a creatively empowering leader, and a collaborative, biblically honoring community.

Another Fatal Team Error

One mistake that causes a team to wither or simply fall apart is to be underchallenged. A lack of challenge drains the soul of a team. There are perhaps few things more frustrating than being on a team that does not know where it is going, that does not jointly feel the stretch of getting there, that is unaware of what challenges and opportunities it faces, and how well it is doing at reaching its goals.

Someone has said that the church today is over taught and underchallenged. This is certainly not true everywhere, but it is piercingly true in far too many churches and church groups. Christianity as we know it today is too often a series of gatherings of people filled with good words instead of vibrant teams and communities full of good works. Yes, we still need pastors and leaders today who will study their Bibles in depth and bring a Word from the Lord, but we also need leaders and teams who will study their communities and the times in which they live and bring a compelling goal from the throne of God that will call together (and to action) a team of believers.

To review and move ahead, here are the first two teaming errors:

Fatal Teaming Error #1: When a team is undervalued.
Fatal Teaming Error #2: When a team is underchallenged.

One of the most important questions for a teaming leader is: Is my team sufficiently challenged? If they are, then their gifts and capacities are being stretched and utilized. If they are not, then the team is, at least in some ways, probably languishing. Atrophy is setting in. But, exactly what causes a team to feel underchallenged?

A team feels underchallenged when the goals of the team are unclear.

A team feels underchallenged when their team leader fails to tap their best ideas and creativity.

A team feels underchallenged when goals are not measured and reviewed frequently.

A team feels underchallenged when team meetings are long, one-sided, and predictable.

A team feels underchallenged when conflicts and differences are left unresolved.

But, what does it take for team leaders to truly challenge their teams to rise to their full potential? And, perhaps more important, what does it take for the team members to challenge one another toward full performance in attitude and accomplishment?

The Blue Angels

One high-performance team known across the country is the Navy Blue Angels. This team of aviators performs aerial acrobatics with their F/A-18 Hornet aircraft. One of the pilots interviewed about the team's high-risk skill and teamwork was asked the question, "What is your goal when you are up there in the air?" He said, "Our goal is to fly perfectly as one. We don't always get it completely perfect, but we strive to always get as close to actually flying as one unit as we possibly can."

What a great goal for a team: "to get as close to flying as one as possible," and in particular for a church or ministry team (even for married couples, for that matter). It was Jesus who set the tone for the teams that would follow him when he prayed for us to his Heavenly Father: "That all of them may be one, Father, just as you are in me and I am in you. May they also be in us so that the world may believe that you have sent me" (John 17:21 NIV).

Group Turned Team

When your group becomes a true team you will find that they move from one perspective or orientation to an entirely different one. As the compelling challenge of a great goal emerges, people's ideas emerge (and merge) as well as their talents and passions. The culture changes. Something electric occurs. The atmosphere takes on new life. A group turns team and, as it does, the people within it thrive and move:

From **me** to **us**

From **several** to **one**

From **rigid** to **nimble**

From **self-will** to **team-will**

From **frustrated** to **focused**

From **leading** to **team leading**

From **empower*ed*** to **empower*ing***

From **controlling** to **collaborating**

From **several paths** to **a common path**

From **a group of individuals** to **a team of team players**

"Committee" Is a Curse Word

Have you ever seen the popular sign that says, "For God so loved the word that he did not send a committee"? That is cute and funny, but it is also true. Jesus did not come to set up a bureaucracy but to call a team of twelve people around him, to train them, and to send them out as a team to turn the world right side up!

One of the first recommendations I have for a church determined to live and act as a teaming church is: if at all possible, get rid of the word "committee." I know that in some cases this may require a change in the verbiage of your church constitution and in some cases it is not possible, but here's my rationale. Many people have come to view committees in churches, and often in businesses and government, as the surefire way to kill any good idea. Unfortunately, they often see a committee as something you "sit" on instead of "serve" with. So, if your congregation and constitution will support it—change from the word *committee* to *teams* or *action groups*. Or, at least, start to informally refer to the committee as a team. If you cannot officially lose the C word, at least determine that you are going to train your committees how to function like true teams. The church will thank you for it.

In what ways do functional committees and vibrant teams tend to differ? Too often, while:

Committees talk about doing things,

Teams actually get things done;

Committees seek to hear every voice,

Teams seek to become one voice;

Committees share their opinions,

Teams share their lives;

Committees have a chairman,

Teams have a coach-leader-facilitator;

Committees take notes,

Teams measure results;

Committees talk about issues,

Teams strategize for results;

(Just one more. Sorry, I couldn't resist sharing this one.)

Committees vegetate,

Teams collaborate.

Ubuntu!

The world champion Boston Celtics (sorry if you're not a fan—I am!) have a tradition that they say helped them win another championship a few years ago. When they break (on the count of three) as a team, they shout, "Ubuntu!"

The word *Ubuntu* hails from Africa and is rich in meaning and significance. Ubuntu is a classical African ethic that, in essence, states and believes: "I am what I am because of who we all are." Or, in other words, my sense of identity is directly connected and related to the community (or team) of which I am a part. Running counter to modern ideas of rugged individualism, Ubuntu challenges the individual to place a deep value on the strength and significance of community.

Desmond Tutu, retired Anglican bishop of Capetown, South Africa, drafted an explanation of Ubuntu in his book:

> A person with Ubuntu is open and available to others, affirming of others, does not feel threatened that others are able and

good, based from a proper self-assurance that comes from knowing that he or she belongs in a greater whole and is diminished when others are humiliated or diminished, when others are tortured or oppressed.[3]

Teaming Is a Mind-Set

People who become great team members and leaders possess a teaming mind-set. The teaming mind-set follows the pattern of Philippians 2, which says "Let each of you look not only to his own interests, but also to the interests of others" (Phil 2:4 ESV). Taking on a teaming mind-set, then, involves obeying the call of Christ to "deny themselves" (Luke 9:23). It requires living life, serving God, working in the church with an attitude that says, "It's not about me!"

Here's an important related statement I posted on Facebook: "There are two kinds of people who walk into a room: those who walk in and say 'Here I am!' and those who walk in and say, 'There YOU are!'"

Sounds pretty good, right? I sure thought so. Just as expected, the first person that responded to the post on Facebook responded with the words: "Love that. . . ." I thought everyone else would respond in similar fashion. But, one person's response on Facebook later that day challenged me to take this thought another step further—an important step. Here's what the person wrote: "Add a third [statement]: 'Here WE are.'"

Wow! "Here WE are." Of course! How simple. How important. How biblical. How did I forget to add that one? Do you want to know "how"? An eleven-letter word: S-E-L-F-I-S-H-N-E-S-S—or, if you prefer, a four-letter word: S-E-L-F. "Self" is the enemy of community, the enemy of the church, the enemy of the kingdom of God and the enemy of biblical teams and teaming.

In order to build great teams, we have to change the way we think. We have to move from "Here I am" and "There you are" to "Here WE are."

Once again, drawing solid circles, or creating great teams, starts with **The Character**; it begins by making sure the team has the right "character," a team with the right kind of people who know how to treat one another in the right way. It is essential that they are honorable and honoring, that they treat one another with honor.

Drawing great team circles together continues with **The Carrot**—this represents helping the team together to find the right kind of challenge to face and to take on. It must be bigger than any one individual and it must be absolutely compelling. It must not only be big enough to convince us that we cannot do it without the other team members and their help, ideally it should also be big enough to convince the team that they cannot do it without God's help!

Team Draw

The word *team* comes from the Latin root *deuk*, which means "to pull" or "to draw." In a real sense, teams are groups of people who pull together to reach a common goal. Church teams or teams of Christ-followers are groups of people who pull together to reach a common goal for the sake of Christ. They are the people pulling not only for their church or organization, but pulling for one another, and pulling for their shared potential in life and ministry.

Teaming is not only an important skill for Christian leaders and workers, it is also fast becoming the skill of the age. The Association of American Colleges and Universities recently commissioned a study to determine the most needed skills for today's graduates to thrive in the current world and economy.

What is the top skill on the list? Innovation?

No.

That is important, but is actually number five on the list.

Number four is *being able to organize information.*

Number three is *oral and written communication.*

Number two is *critical thinking and reasoning.*

And number one on the list is *teamwork skills*!

That's right. To be specific, the report cited "teamwork skills and the ability to collaborate with others in diverse group settings."

What does that mean?

Keep reading!

Drawing Your Circle

Questions to Ask Your Team

1. How can you tell when a group of people truly becomes a team? What characterizes that change?

2. Do you agree that collaboration is a primary skill needed in this age? What does genuine collaboration require of us?

34

3. Was the early church collaborative? Explain.

4. Does your team feel overchallenged or underchallenged?

5. Do you tend to be a person who says "Here I am" or "There you are" when you walk into a room?

6. What will it require of us to adopt more of a "Here WE are" mindset in our lives and ministry?

Chapter Two

The Team Tour: Great Teams and Teaming Players

No one can whistle a symphony;
it takes an orchestra to play it.
—H. E. Luccock

The days are long gone when I can think up a sermon by myself.
—Anonymous Pastor, Megachurch

Jesus never sent anyone out to do anything alone; at least, I cannot find an instance in the Gospels in which he did so. He started his ministry by simply building a community of net fishermen. When he sent these disciples out to towns and villages, he sent them two by two. When he sent them to wait on the coming of the Holy Spirit, he sent 120 of them to a place of prayer in Jerusalem. Even when the first missionaries were commissioned in the book of Acts, there were two leaders and one protégé sent out to cast the net and spread the kingdom of God.

Jesus' purpose in coming to earth, according to Luke's Gospel, was "to seek and to save the lost" (Luke 19:10 NIV). Jesus' primary strategy to accomplish this purpose was to build a team. The most pivotal leadership decision he made was the people he chose as his disciples. After the much-prayed-about selection, he called them to be "with him" (Mark 3:14). He invested the better part of three years working with his team, teaching, sharing, training, talking, confronting, eating, traveling, and serving others. Pondering how he built his team is a worthwhile leadership exercise. As we draw wisdom from the inspired words of Christ, we draw a model worth following from his ways.

Observing Great Teams

One of the best ways to build a stronger team is to spend time with, and learn more about, strong teams and team leaders; to get in the trenches with people who have learned to be teaming leaders. Observation is an irreplaceable training ground.

There are all kinds of teams that exist in every sphere of life—from NASCAR pit crews to Navy SEAL units to Olympic hockey teams to church and ministry teams. Those who take the time to observe them get the principles and practices of great teams down, and they benefit. Many do not, and as a result, they struggle.

So, let's go on a little tour. Let's hop on the observation bus and take a closer look at some incredible teams.

Team Graham

One of the strongest ministry teams of the twentieth century was arguably Billy Graham's band of servant-leaders. The famed evangelist is quick to note that critical to his effectiveness in ministry has been the group of men with whom he collaborated and that supported him for so many years. Key among them were men such as Cliff Barrows and the late T. W. Wilson.

After Wilson passed way, several of his friends and admirers noted how unusually capable and gifted he was and how he had sacrificed a public ministry of his own in order to support his friend and colleague, Billy Graham. Cliff Barrows, long-time associate of Graham's, told *Christianity Today* that Wilson "had a great gift as an evangelist, but he gave that up for what he felt was a higher responsibility when Billy asked him to travel with him."

> Paul Robbins and Harold Myra, long-term co-leaders of [*Christianity Today*], compared Wilson's sacrificial willingness to serve to that of General George C. Marshall. Marshall led the joint chiefs of the armed services under Franklin Roosevelt. Perhaps the best military mind of his time, Marshall longed to direct the cross-Channel Allied invasion of Europe. But ever the servant-leader, Marshall sacrificed battlefield glory to stay in Washington, where the president wanted and needed him. Instead, Dwight D. Eisenhower won the glory of victory, and eventually gained the presidency that could have been Marshall's.[1]

Graham was no solitary figure. The phrase "the Billy Graham Team" has become a legend and virtually synonymous with Graham's legacy. Many say that one of his wisest decisions was surrounding himself with a strong team. He had a team of men who surrendered their individual goals and dreams to the call they felt to a team ministry. Barrows once said, "Life is not a solo existence. Effective work in evangelism is not a solo ministry. It is a team of people whose hearts God has knit together."

William Martin, a biographer of Graham, said:

> Unquestionably, part of the success of the Graham team has been the ability of the individuals involved to subordinate their egos for the good of the ministry as a whole. They all subordinated themselves to the ministry, not just [to] Billy Graham. And he subordinated himself to them and the ministry, as well. Of course, the team had a leader, but the leader never thought he was the only important member.[2]

New Forms of Working Together

There has been an increasing acknowledgment in recent years among church leaders of the great need for finding new forms of working together, of teaming and community. Within several growing local churches, a reemergence of interest and experimentation with a team approach to leadership has emerged. Through wider spread acknowledgement of the dynamics of postmodernism and other social transitions, including globalization, secularization, pluralism, and others, it is becoming clear that hierarchical models of leadership and authority have lost their traction and effectiveness. Nancy Ortberg, a teambuilding specialist and former Bible teacher at Willow Creek Community Church, says, "Leadership is becoming more collaborative and less hierarchical." Thomas Bandy acknowledges, "The paradigm for church life in the 21st century will not be the corporate paradigm but the *mission-team* paradigm."

Team Northland

When Joel Hunter was asked to come to an independent church in Orlando, Florida, he left the United Methodist church he pastored in Greenwood, Indiana. For several nights before accepting the call, Hunter recalls waking up with his "heart all disturbed" and with the feeling that God wanted him to move. Soon thereafter, he and his wife moved to Northland Community Church in Orlando, Florida. The couple eventually discovered that the elders' wives at Northland had prayed that God would "disturb the heart" of the pastor he wanted to come and lead the church.

In 1985, Northland had a congregation of about two hundred. Over the past twenty years, it has grown to some fifteen thousand attendees. At one point, the church intentionally made a change from the moniker of "community church" to "a church distributed." This new change moved the congregational efforts outside of their walls and used creative technologies to link with worshipers across town and across the globe.

While technology is a tool at Northland, the genius behind their strategy is team and teaming leadership. The church is knit together and networked by teams. For instance, there is a Worship Service Team made up of twelve people. At the hub of the church is the Pastoral Leadership Team, which is made up of three leaders, including Hunter.

"The team structure at Northland is very fluid," says Hunter.

> Simply put: I am the vision guy. I need people to help me oversee and manage the details. I am a big picture person. Then, our worship pastor is our relationship guy, the second guy on the team. He is intuitive and very connected to people. But, we both play a vital part on the team.
>
> The third person on our team is expert at the arrangement of details. I mean it is incredible to see all of the things he is able to manage. He has the ability to connect the dots of all that we are doing and to make sure nothing falls through the cracks.

According to Hunter there are two things that keep his lead team strong: laughter and mutual deference. He says,

> We just enjoy each other. We laugh all the time. And, we value each other's expertise. I am good at things they are not, and vice versa. Somehow the team, the relationship, and the partnership just works. Our team has become kind of a central team at the church that others seek to emulate. People can tell how much the three of us enjoy working and serving together.

Team Willow Creek

One of the most longstanding megachurches in America is Willow Creek Community Church in South Barrington, Illinois. From the start, Willow Creek has embraced the value of teaming leadership and of the teaming church. It was among the first large churches in the country to incorporate a preaching team.

Nancy Ortberg recounts her tenure at Willow Creek, which has been organized around teams or teaming communities since its earliest years:

Of the top ten things I learned at Willow, one of them was that we didn't treat volunteers any different than our paid staff members. They were valued and held to the same standards. All of us were ministers—some were considered "paid staff" and everyone else "unpaid staff." Expectations were the same! Everywhere you went at Willow, you ended up on a team.

Willow Creek has also led the way in partnering with the business community in the ongoing pursuit of understanding the subject of effective leadership. Willow hosts a leadership summit every August that has drawn upon the insights of such nonecclesiastical leaders as former President Bill Clinton, Jack Welch, and Bono.

The value that seems to fuel Willow's irresistible interest in the business community is clearly evangelism, but also the idea that all truth is God's truth. In his treatise *On Christian Teaching*, Augustine wrote:

> A person who is a good and true Christian should realize that *truth belongs to his Lord, wherever it is found*, gathering and acknowledging it even in pagan literature, but rejecting superstitious vanities and deploring and avoiding those who "though they knew God did not glorify him as God."

With Augustine's theory of truth in mind, I went on a two-year-long search to discover more of the truths about teams in various fields and forms. In addition to studying how teams have worked, and too often not worked, in the church, some of the other areas I pursued included teams and teaming leadership in the field of sports, the military, education, even NASCAR, and the world of business.

Teambuilding in Business

In recent years, teaming and teambuilding have gained their most notable acclaim in the business community. They have become essential organizational components and strategies. The concept of teamwork is fast becoming synonymous with successful management in today's business organizations.

The U.S. Department of Labor reported the strength of this trend of teams in the business community and recently identified teamwork as one of the five workplace skills that should be "more aggressively taught in public schools."[3] "The report suggests that teaching these new skills is necessary both for the success of individuals in job settings and for the success of U.S. companies competing with foreign and domestic rivals."[4] "Our organizations are more complex and more competitive. No longer can we depend upon a few peak performers to rise to the top to lead. If we are to survive we must figure out ways to tap the creativity and (the) potential of people at all levels."[5]

Additionally, "In a study of 179 companies by the Mercer Management consulting firm, 69% of those who used teams extensively said they planned to increase their reliance on teams in the next three years."[6] In a sense, most work in our world is fast becoming teamwork.

The Greatest Teaming Leader Ever

A maxim that rings consistently true in the corporate world is that "teams outperform individuals."[7] Vast corporations such as General Electric have implemented companywide teambuilding and management efficiency strategies such as Six Sigma. Noted business consultants and specialists such as Ken Blanchard have even come to recognize that current business team applications and governing principles were established millennia ago in the Old Testament and in the early church as recorded in ancient biblical literature. Here is what Blanchard, notably one of the most sought-after business consultants in the world, concluded about teams:

> Today, as never before in history, organizational leaders are realizing that to maximize performance people need to be organized in teams. No longer can we depend upon a few peak performers to make the difference. The mantra today is "none of us is as smart as all of us."
>
> People who "get" the importance of teamwork and are breaking new ground in the area of teambuilding, often think of themselves as creative innovators. That's what I used to think . . . That was all before I began to study Jesus as a leader. I soon discovered that everything I ever wrote about or taught Jesus did. All I was doing was rediscovering what He had already proven as simple truths about working with people.
>
> How was this possible? Easy! Jesus was the greatest leader of all time. Regardless of your religious persuasion, you have to admit that Jesus was an incredible leader. He hired twelve incompetent guys. None of His disciples had any experience in becoming "fishers of men." The only one with any real education was Judas, and he was Jesus' only turnover problem. And yet, with this diverse, seemingly ragtag group, Jesus changed the world forever.[8]

Although teams and teaming strategies have resurfaced in the business community in the past couple of decades, they have actually been around for centuries. "Teams have existed for hundreds of years, are the subject of countless books, and have been celebrated throughout many countries and cultures."[9]

Seven Powerful Principles from Business Teams

Here are a few key principles of teams and teambuilding that emerge in the foremost business literature available on this subject. In light of Augustine's view of truth, several, if not all, of them are effectively translatable in efforts of church development and team ministry mobilization.

First, teaming is the best strategy for building an organization in such a time of great cultural diversity and complexity as the twenty-first century.

Jon R. Katzenbach and Douglas K. Smith, in their highly acclaimed book *The Wisdom of Teams*, acknowledge that "a real team—appropriately focused and rigorously disciplined—is the most versatile unit organizations have for meeting both performance and change challenges in today's complex world."[10] In the final analysis, the "team remains the most flexible and the most powerful unit of performance, learning, and change in any organization."[11] From exhaustive research, Patrick Lencioni came to this vital conclusion regarding teams and teamwork: "Teamwork is almost always lacking within organizations that fail, and *often* present within those that succeed."[12]

Second, teams are not built by merely having meetings but by a group of people collectively facing great projects, compelling goals, and shared tasks.

It isn't so much the teaming guidelines or the team leader's efforts at inspiration that turn a group into a functioning team. More so, it is a great and shared goal that motivates people to form effective teams.[13]

Effectively communicated goals are characteristically measurable and challenging enough to stretch a bunch of rugged individuals into a performance team. Great goals pull us out of ourselves and into the necessary realms of collaboration and interdependence. They transform us from laborers to *co*-laborers—or, to coin a term, into "collaboratives." As it turns out, the positive pressure of a challenging goal is a good (and essential) motivator: "Someone given a stretch goal will often be forced to seek out and interact with more people than someone whose goal is set at a much lower level."[14] Great teams need great goals to be greatly challenged to meet (or exceed) them.

> Challenges create teams, not [merely] the desire to be a team. . . . A demanding performance challenge tends to create a team. The hunger for performance is far more important to team success than team-building exercises, special incentives, or team leaders with ideal profiles. In fact, teams often form around such challenges without any help or support from management. Conversely, potential teams without such challenges usually fail to become teams.[15]

One mistake many organizations make is overusing static (or permanent) teams and underusing temporary teams. Amy Edmondson, professor at Harvard Business School, says that smart organizations frequently

> gather experts in temporary groups to solve problems. . . . When companies need to accomplish something that hasn't been done before, . . . a leader's emphasis has to shift from composing and managing teams to inspiring and enabling teaming.[16]

When opportunities and challenges emerge and the clock is ticking, there is no better proven way to engage them than with a well-qualified and diversely gifted temporary team. The challenge of great expectation and limited time can bring a team together and draw out team brilliance. It is during these short-term assignments that team and team members' capacities are recognized and where the eagles on your team are given a chance to soar.

Third, not every need or opportunity faced by an organization calls for a team approach.

There are some tasks or projects that simply are better handled by an individual. In these particular cases, a team approach could slow down the work and even impede progress. For instance, I attended a church staff meeting years ago where the team leader brought in the church bulletin and we spent almost two hours evaluating how it looked. In my opinion, this turned out to be a grand waste of time for one main reason— only one out of about eight members of the team had any experience with graphic art or design. It turned out to be one big opinion-fest, with little accomplished.

Katzenbach and Smith see it this way:

The most effective performance units are those that understand which goals require a single leader and which require a performing team. . . . We now believe that any performance situation that warrants a team effort must meet three litmus tests: (1) the need for collective work products to be delivered by two or more people working together in real time; (2) leadership roles that need to shift among the members; and (3) the need for mutual accountability in addition to individual accountability.[17]

Fourth, teams are smarter than individuals; a lot smarter.[18]

While hierarchical leaders focus on how much they as individuals know, teaming leaders focus much more on what they don't know and search for ways to fill that breach through teaming with a qualified group of gifted individuals. Teaming leaders are never know-it-alls; on the contrary, they are people who stay interested and curious.

James Surowiecki, in his book *The Wisdom of Crowds*, says:

> The best CEOs . . . recognize the limits of their own knowledge and of individual decision-making. That's why important decisions at [General Motors], in the days when it was the most successful corporation in the world, were made by what Alfred Sloan called "group management." And it's why legendary business thinker Peter Drucker has said, "The smart CEOs methodically build a management team around them."[19]

Teams are smarter than individuals for several reasons. In The Information Age, there are simply too many facts to be considered for one person to process all of it alone. Added team members are like added gigabytes of memory in your computer. You can process more information more rapidly and effectively (or, in church terms, wisely; Prov 15:22). Additionally, too much emphasis on individual credentials and accomplishments creates significant blind spots in an organization. Finally, teams provide a think tank of support before making any significant and sweeping decisions. The Bible says the same thing in a different way: "For lack of guidance a nation falls, / but many advisers make victory sure" (Prov 11:14 NIV).

Fifth, a teaming approach helps create a culture of truthfulness and candor, where knowledge, insights, conflicts, and potentials are not ignored, but rather, honestly and regularly acknowledged.

More business leaders today are recognizing that candor is an essential resource in today's competitive and fast markets. The fact is that well-developed teams with their collective analytical powers will more quickly and accurately assess the truth about a situation, a problem, or an opportunity.[20]

John's Gospel says that Jesus was "full of grace and *truth*" (John 1:14, italics mine). Team members have to be taught to value, if not love, the truth, the hard truth. This will require training and experience on the job since many, if not most, people in today's work environments are instead taught to avoid the truth, especially if the truth is hard to face or when it may generate unwelcomed conflict. Such a sea change in corporate culture is not an easy process and requires much deliberate effort to establish and to nourish.

Former CEO of General Electric, Jack Welch, summed it up well in his book, *Winning*:

> Classic philosophers like Immanuel Kant give powerful arguments for the view that not being candid is actually about self-interest—making your *own* life easier. . . . Kant had another point, too. He said that people are often strongly tempted not to be candid because they don't look at the big picture. They worry that when they speak their minds and the news isn't good, they stand a strong chance of alienating other people. But what they don't see is that lack of candor is the ultimate form of alienation. "There was a huge irony in this for Kant," [Bauer] says. "He believed that when people avoid candor in order to curry favor with other people, they actually destroy trust, and in that way, ultimately erode society [i.e., community]."[21]

Sixth, the best teams are those who are encouraged to connect both inside and outside of the regular team meetings.

As it turns out, the latest research (from *Harvard Business Review*) shows that "social time [among team members] turns out to be deeply critical to team performance, often accounting for more than 50% of positive changes in communication patterns."[22] A team's productivity is best determined by the "energy and engagement" they share outside their formal meetings.[23]

The research revealed that when organizations allowed their employees to have the same break time their overall productivity increased significantly. Even changes in the size of tables in break room areas, more conducive to small group interaction, led to a marked improvement in team cohesion and effectiveness.

Seventh, and not least important of all, effective teaming requires a new kind of leader, a teaming leader.

"Today's leader must be an enabler of people and a facilitator of teams—not only as an effective team leader but as an effective team member as well."[24] Today's church and corporate leader must understand and use people development, people empowerment, and coaching skills. Within the metaphor of the circle, consider this: "The measure of a powerful person is that their circle of influence is greater than their circle of control."[25] In chapter 6 we take a closer look at the characteristics and practices of a teaming leader.

The Uniqueness of a Ministry Team

As mentioned earlier, there are numerous insights we can draw from team and teambuilding literature in numerous fields and disciplines, including business teams. However, although many valuable principles and techniques are contained within these resources, the motivation and foundation for such teams and teambuilding can easily become one-dimensional. The purpose of forming teams in the business community is often primarily to improve the efficiency of the corporation, the flow of communication, and ultimately, the financial bottom line. Although there are instances emerging of newfound interpersonal and even spiritual benefits within the workplace to using teams, profits are often seen solely in the material benefits afforded by this approach.

Erwin McManus wrote:

> Whenever we see the church through the template of an organization, we begin creating an institution. When we relate to the church as an organism, [however] we begin to awaken an apostolic ethos, which unleashes the movement of God. The power and life of God's Spirit working in his people result in nothing less than cultural transformation.[26]

In the case of many business or sports teams, the "good" of team is seen merely in the performance or production that flows out of such a group. Even noted management guru Peter Drucker has written, "Teams . . . are tools. As such, each team design has its own uses, its own characteristics, its own limitation. Teamwork is neither 'good' nor 'desirable'— it is a fact. Wherever people work together or play together they do so as a team."[27]

One clear distinction between biblical teams in the church and community and business teams in the marketplace is their inherent cohesion, value, and significance. For the most part business teams are valued solely on their ability to get the work of that business done and to help generate a profit. This observation is not to deny the inherent godliness of productivity. In fact, Deuteronomy 8:18 says, "remember the LORD your God, for it is he who gives you the ability to produce wealth, and so confirms his covenant" (NIV). But, church teams exist for something far more important than productivity or profit.

The church team finds value in the accomplishment of the church's mission and in the process of teaming itself, as it is a reflection of the Trinity and, thus, a way for Christ-followers to unite in purpose and service and to somehow reflect the glory of God. This is a clear distinction of a true church team.

Another distinction of a biblical team is that when it is functioning properly, it can become an answer to Christ's prayer for unity in John 17. Since the prayer Jesus offered to the Father in John 17 on behalf of the church was that they all become as "one," a ministry team is a place where men and women can help answer this prayer. Jesus' prayer was specifically "that all of them may be one, Father, just as you are in me and I am in you" (v. 21 NIV). In his prayer, Jesus called not only for unity in the church but also the same kind of unity that he shares with his Father and with the Spirit in the Trinitarian union. The pooling of the lives, souls, gifts, and energies of men and women together in ministry emulates the collaborations of the Trinity itself and becomes another picture of the declaration that as in heaven, so on earth. It is a forceful reflection of the glory of God, and the nature of God, on earth.

Finally, a biblical team is a reflection of Jesus' strategy for building the church; it represents doing his will, his way. Jesus poured himself into twelve men that together formed a ministry team. He chose them to be "with him" (Mark 3:14). In like manner, the apostle Paul followed the example of Christ. He reflected Jesus' strategy and urged Timothy, his young protégé, to do the same: "And the things you have heard me say in the presence of many witnesses entrust to reliable men who will also be qualified to teach others" (2 Tim 2:2 NIV).

Community developed on a team can cause that team to realize incredible accomplishments. Also, it can build a more lasting longevity. Bill Hybels tells a story of how he observed this in the Billy Graham evangelistic team on a visit to the evangelist's home in North Carolina.

> Several years ago, I was invited to Washington, D.C., to attend the ceremony where Dr. Billy Graham would receive the Congressional

Medal of Honor. The Capitol Rotunda was filled with scores of government officials and dozens of world leaders. The ceremony was patriotic, stately, and very honoring. When Dr. Graham stood to receive the medal, he looked at the award and then said quietly, "This medal is really not for me. This medal is for our team. We've been together for forty-five years. Without each member my life would not have been the same. I owe them so much." Then he listed, one by one, the names of those who had formed the core of his evangelistic ministry. As he spoke their names he struggled to contain his emotion.

Still, I did not fully realize how deeply Dr. Graham and his associates valued team until, sometime later, I enjoyed a visit with him at his home in Montreat, North Carolina. He led me down the hill from his home and pointed out the houses being built nearby by some of his team members. Apparently, forty-five years of togetherness was not enough for this tightly knit team. Even as they neared the end of their lives, they wanted to be together, caring for and supporting each other, just as they had throughout their ministry years. I was deeply moved by their commitment to stay together all the way to the end.[28]

From the fields of battle to the marketplaces of trade and commerce to the pastoring fields of ministry, teams are the primary means that help people partner together to get the job done. While the business community is quite developed in this area, the church has some lost ground to recover. In fact, it may be that the practical and theological significance of developing true ministry teams is one of the most untapped church resources today.

But what are the essentials of a great ministry team? Of those teams that get the most done within the most God-honoring circles or environments, just what are they made of? What is their distinctive? What is their team DNA?

A Teaming Leader Interview, Medium-Sized Church: Joe Lyons

Joe Lyons, pastor, Bentonville First Assembly, Bentonville, Arkansas, www.bentonvillefirst.com.

Q: How long have you pastored this church?

A: Two-and-a-half years.

Q: What is your average weekly attendance currently?

A: 460.

Q: How important and integral are teams and teambuilding to your church?

A: Vital.

Q: What role have they played throughout its history so far and what role do they play today?

A: It is my understanding that Bentonville First did not have a history of team-led ministries. For the past two years our entire structure has been based on teams. Paid staff and volunteer staff operate in a team structure. I have found the team concept identifies emerging leaders, strategic training, effective communication, efficient processes, and firm structure.

Q: What would you say makes for a great ministry team?

A: Competent team members who fully leverage the strengths of each member.

Q: What does it take to turn a group of people into a real team?

A: It takes a great leader to lead the group and model through brainstorming, strategies, and processes that value each individual's contributions. This develops a greater appreciation for what we can do together than independently. Teams are developed. A group of people who call themselves a team will not automatically function as a team.

Q: How can you tell when that happens?

A: You know this has happened when the experience has been fulfilling for the team and all members are excited about the next task.

Q: What characterizes the most effective team players at your church? What does it take to be a great team player?

A: A desire that each team player brings their "A" game so that the team has produced their best effort.

Q: How important is a great goal to a great team?

A: For a goal to truly be a great goal it must align with the mission and vision of the church. A great team is challenged to rise to the occasion by goals that are bigger than their current capabilities. Great goals will inspire great teams to stretch, recruit others to the team, and include the God factor. Mediocre goals produce mediocre results. Insignificant goals breed boredom and lethargy.

Q: What have you come to understand about teams and team leadership today?

A: People want to be on team if they are led by strong leaders. If you want to attract and keep great leaders you must address and redirect weak leaders. They will not coexist long term. Teams are always evolving. The team structure must be flexible. You must have strategic forward-thinking leaders.

Q: Have the ingredients of a great ministry team at your church changed as the church has grown? Explain.

A: Change is required for continued growth. We have found that for approximately every one hundred new congregants, our teams experience growth, restructure, or transition of some sort. Momentum is lost when the growth pattern of the church outgrows the growth pattern of the ministry teams. This includes all ministry teams from the departmental teams to pastoral teams.

Drawing Your Circle

Questions to Ask Your Team

1. What characterizes a great team?

2. Ken Blanchard says that Jesus was the greatest teambuilder who ever lived. How did Jesus build teams?

3. Are teams and teambuilding more needed now than at other times in history? Explain.

4. Is a teaming approach the right way to get the work of the church done? How so?

5. Are teams smarter than individuals? Explain.

6. What are the main differences between business teams and ministry teams?

Chapter Three

The DNA of a Winning Team

The health and long-term effectiveness of any ministry begins
with the health and unity of its primary leadership teams.
—*Larry Osbourne, Lead Pastor, North Coast Church, San Diego*

If you have too many people wired like you on the team—you're in trouble.
—*Kent Ingle, President, Southeastern University*

What is the stuff of great ministry teams? What are they made of? What practices and values fuel their ongoing effectiveness? In other words, what is the DNA of a winning team?

Rick Warren says, "The church is a body, not a business. It is an organism, not an organization! It is a family to be loved, not a machine to be engineered, and not a company to be managed."[1]

Craig Groeschel says, "A great team is a collection of great people with different gifts but the same mission."

The Teaming Church Principle says, "To become a great team your group must have a deeply challenging goal, a creatively empowering leader, and a collaborative, biblically honoring community."

Pastors and church leaders are not only commissioned to call people to Christ but also to call them more fully into the body of Christ. Jesus did not tell Peter, "I will build up my individual servants," but rather, "I will build my church" (that is, my *ekklesia,* or my called-out ones). The wise pastor and teaming leader will not just recruit people to work on a team in order to complete a project. This is not a team, but a task force. Rather, they will more intentionally see the team environment not as mere recruitment, but engagement. The process is much more significant. The passionate and sincere leader sees it as calling people into a collaborative community that represents the body of Christ, something altogether different than mere recruitment. There is a difference between merely completing a task and reflecting the glory of God.

Many churches and church leaders today are rediscovering the essential community dynamics of the gospel. We are called to worship together, to pray together, to serve together, to witness together, and to work together. Teaming approaches to leadership, work, and worship are also receiving enthusiastic response from today's communities and businesses, as well, and they are serving practical uses. Best of all, church and church leaders are rediscovering the spiritual power of community and collaboration. They are finding that God has called us to live as one for more than one reason. The church is becoming more intentional about community.

That is a good thing.

Team DNA

The Human Genome Project has taught us much about our physiological design and potential strengths and weaknesses. Learning more about our individual DNA is leading to multiple scientific and medical breakthroughs. In a sense it is showing us that much of what we will become in life is already preprogrammed into our biological and physiological makeup. Whereas the race to the moon of the last century created a fascination with the universe above, scientific breakthrough and the human genome is now creating a similar fascination with the universe (or *you*-niverse) within.

When a team is formed, it too has somewhat of a latent DNA. The particular assortment of people who form a team have a unique potential comprised of what the various team members collectively bring to the team and the unique potential it offers. No two teams are the same. It is often fascinating and sometimes frustrating to see, but different groups of people tend to form different types of teams.

More and more, neurologists are learning that our brains have been designed to not only think and work with some measure of individuality and independence but also to work together with others. We are even discovering that among the estimated one hundred billion neurons in our brains, we also have a particular type of neuron referred to as "mirror neurons" that are keenly in tune with the people around us. Some experts say that mirror neurons function almost like a neurological wi-fi that tracks and attracts the collaborations of those around us. The bottom line is this scientific discovery mirrors what the Bible has revealed for thousands of years: we have been formed for community and collaboration. We are never at our best without it. We were not only made for a dream and a team, we were hardwired for it!

Randolph Bourne confirmed this idea several years ago in a book he wrote called *Youth and Life*. He said, "A man with few friends (or colleagues) is only half-developed. There are whole sides to his personality that can only be called out by friends; they can only be developed by deep and meaningful collaborations."[2] There is something about being around friends or with a team that challenges you in ways you cannot challenge yourself. "Iron sharpens iron, / and one man sharpens another" (Prov 27:17 ESV).

The fact is that you and I possess leadership and creative potential within our minds and hearts that can only be stirred up and drawn out by our friends, coworkers, and collaborative communities. You can never be at your best alone. To be at your best, you must be a part of a team. Once teams start to form then the person and person-*ality* of that team also forms, in much the same manner as an individual person develops. Every time a team is formed, or *re*-formed by the addition of a new member, the DNA of that particular combination of lives takes on a new shape with new (and unique) potential.

Discovering Team DNA

But, just what will it take to tap into the team DNA that resides within a particular set of people? Here are three traits that must be continuously encouraged, examined, and developed in order to bring out the best a team has to offer. When it comes to the disciplines, or regular practices, of a team, these are three essentials:

- Deep Trust
- No Elephants
- Accountability to the Team

Let's take a brief look at each one of these and consider how they can each help to tap team potential.

Deep Trust: Winning Teams Collaborate!

Another essential component of an effective team is trust among the members of the team. The team leader must trust his team members and they need to trust the leader. Also, there must be a trust that exists between the various team members in order for the necessary level of confidence required to accomplish great things together. John Kotter says,

> Teamwork . . . can be created in many different ways. But regardless of the process used, one component is necessary: trust. When trust is present, you will usually be able to create teamwork. When it is missing, you won't.[3]

As with individual relationships, trust is built every time team members and leaders keep their commitments and promises. It is strengthened each time a timeline item is promptly met and upon every team "win," no matter how small or preliminary in nature the victory. Trust is the goodwill that exists among people on a team who are confident in their own abilities and in the abilities of the team itself. Trust can, at first, be given, but in order to be maintained, it must consistently be earned. When trust is broken, rebuilding it can be a long and tedious process. Trust is a team essential.

Patrick Lencioni, noted team specialist and author, says:

> When it comes to teams, trust is all about vulnerability. Team members who trust one another learn to be comfortable being open, even exposed, to one another around their failures, weaknesses, even fears. . . . The key ingredient to building trust is not time. It is courage.[4]

Trust is probably the most oft-mentioned and common ingredient within great ministry teams. Experts from all fields of teambuilding agree on this essential. All team values have their roots in trust or team trust. For example, honesty is an essential team value, but on what is it founded? It is founded on trust. In order for me to be honest with my teammate, it is essential that I feel that I can trust him or her.

But how is trust developed? Where does it come from? How can it be nurtured? And, how does a group of people learn to trust their team leaders and one another? It's simple, but challenging: team trust is a process. It takes time, but it is something that is built and added to with every task accomplished, every promise kept and every concern addressed.

A warning: trust is much more quickly lost than it is built. Building trust is a patient process, one day and one step at a time.

Faithfulness and trust go hand in hand. This is also true on a team. Team leaders and members often want their teammates to quickly pour their trust into a latest idea or plan, but trust is something that grows over time and amidst the journey of dreaming. It is a sacred trust; hard fought for, but well worth the effort. It is earned by consistency of character and behavior, by planning, and the accomplishment of team goals together.

While a decision to trust the team with a short-term plan or idea is one thing, developing the deep trust required to accomplish great goals and to see God build great ministries and a great church is yet another. Deep trust will take deep time and deep and faithful action to develop. But, it is absolutely worth it!

Here are some things that build trust on a team:

- Promises made and kept.
- Intent, focused, and reflective listening to each person's ideas and opinions.
- Ongoing mutual concern for team members' personal needs and families.
- Remembering special occasions in your team members' lives.
- Straight and honest talk.
- Loyalty to the team and team members.
- Emotional honesty. (When you're glad about something—let them know; when you are angry—let them know.)
- Accurate reporting. (No skewing or fudging of numbers.)

Here are some of the things that erode trust on a team:

- Cloaked confrontations. (Those times in which you really want to confront one particular team member, but instead in the name of convenience or cowardice you confront the entire team and leave everyone to try to figure out for just whom it was meant.)
- Unnecessarily long team meetings. (Wasting team members' time because you haven't planned out your own well enough.)
- Delaying commitments.
- Talking critically about a team member when the person is not present to respond.
- Postponing decision making without good reason.
- Unkept promises.

Make no mistake. People deeply desire to work in an environment of trust. A team that wants to accomplish reasonable goals has to have the ingredient of trust. A team that wants to accomplish exceptional goals must have an exceptional sense of trust. Perhaps the most important question that team members, and potential team members, ask about their team leader is, can I trust that person?

Collaboration and Communication

While trust is essential to a truly collaborative environment, it is important to remember that in order to collaborate you must COMMUNICATE. According to the *Harvard Business Review* article, "The New Science of Building Great Teams," "The key to high performance lay not in the content of a team's discussions but in the manner in which it was communicating."[5]

So, in order to build an environment of great trust not only is it important that a team communicate but also the way they do so is vital. An honoring circle is one that frees teams and team members to speak openly, honestly, and passionately.

The article goes on to suggest that talent is overrated in choosing team members. It is far more strategic "to learn how they communicate and to shape and guide the team so that it follows successful communication patterns."[6]

No Elephants—Winning Teams Are Candid!

Few things are more frustrating than sitting in on a team meeting and listening to the leader talk about everything but the very issue you know is the most pressing (and the most felt) one of the moment. Sometimes a team will experience a rift or a division that brings hurt, confusion, and disgruntled emotion into the atmosphere. The temptation of leadership is to avoid acknowledging the elephant in the room, to just ignore him, to pretend he doesn't exist, and hope he will just leave on his own, or to attempt to move ahead with discussions, plans, and dreams in a business-as-usual approach. When these moments occur, the emotional elephant is so present and so real that it is virtually impossible for team members to focus on the tasks or challenges at hand.

Some of the potential elephants that show up among teams and team meetings are:

- Unresolved tensions;
- Incomplete discussions;
- Unkept promises;
- Unclear roles;
- Inadequate communication;
- Unclear measurements;
- Uncertain goals;
- Insufficiently oriented new team members;
- Overly controlling leadership actions; and
- Compromises of team values.

Great teams and team members are not just aware of the elephants, they are elephant hunters! They regularly chase them down. They know that the elephants in the room, the unresolved issues and poor communications, are enemies of teams and teaming; they know that untended, they can take the life, fun, and motivation right out of the room, and right out of the team.

A newborn elephant weighs about 150 pounds. And baby elephants begin walking within fifteen minutes after their birth. The same is true of the proverbial elephants in the room. When you allow an unresolved or unacknowledged issue to enter your team environment, it will grow incredibly fast and start walking around and bumping into people as soon as it is born. Great teams will not tolerate elephants in the room.

So, learn to be a great elephant hunter. Sniff them out and deal with them swiftly. Sometimes the conflict and dialog produced by elephant hunting will cause issues and truths to come to the surface that are at first awkward, but are absolutely key to the development of the team, church, and of the mission.

Elephant hunting requires a few sharpened skills such as candor, confrontation, and conviction. Candor is probably the biggest missing element on most teams. The lack of it keeps many teams from ever becoming truly great. The team that can learn to balance the grace of honor and the skill of candor will find an incredible sweet spot from which to lead and influence others. We analyze candor more in chapter 6. But for now, it is important to recognize that candor is full-out honesty, an ability to call the challenge and the conflict for what it truly is.

Confrontation is an essential art for ministering in the age of collaboration. Long gone is the political effectiveness of being nice. Leaders cannot nice their way through a conflict. Elephants just don't respond to niceness, they require staring down and sharpshooting. But, there is a preferred way to confront them.

Affirmation—Confrontation—Reaffirmation

When confronting a team or team member, first you should *affirm* your commitment to them and the value you place on them as individuals. Second, *confront* them with clarity and absolute honesty. Call the issue and the conflict for what it truly is. Get it fully in your scopes and describe exactly what you see. Then, once the confrontation is communicated, make sure to *reaffirm* the person or persons you are confronting.

Conviction is the soul fuel required to hunt elephants. It takes courage, but the more you practice confrontation with honor, the greater ease you will develop. Confrontation is never fun, but hunting elephants actually can be. It can be absolutely invigorating and renewing at times for your team. Clearing the team atmosphere and environment of unwanted predators can help fortify the solidarity of your team and team members. Robert Cooley has one of the best definitions I have heard of what leaders do. "Leaders do two things: they *frame issues* and *engage conflicts.*" You frame the issue when you get the elephant in your sights. You engage the conflict when you confront it!

Accountable to the Team— Winning Teams Are Committed!

One of the most powerful assets of a teaming approach to church and ministry is team accountability. However, probably one of the most draining aspects of leadership for many pastors today is the need to hold everyone who reports to them, if not everyone in the entire church, accountable. But, just what does that mean? And, what does that look like?

Accountability is connected to the sense of responsibility that we want all our employees, staff members, and volunteers to feel in their roles within the church. The old saying goes, "You cannot expect what you do not inspect." If that is true, and I believe it is, a hierarchical model of leadership is a problem. One person cannot adequately observe and monitor the effectiveness of several, much less dozens, of people at once.

The Team as Person

Developing a solid sense of accountability among team members requires looking at the team or church you serve in a different way. In the business world, there is an organizational concept known as "the organization as person." The idea of this concept is that one healthy way to evaluate an organization (in this case, the church or ministry team you serve) is to view it as a person, as one entity or one living being. In a sense, this is what Paul the leader was doing when he referred to the entire church as a singular entity called the body of Christ (1 Cor 12:12).

It helps to think and talk in terms of team member commitment to the church or ministry as a person. The apostle Paul did so. He referred to the church as not many, but one, bride—the bride of Christ. Apparently in his ministry and work with churches, it helped Paul to look at the church as a person, as the body of Christ, as a bride, not merely as an organization or a business. Such a view of the church or ministry team as person helps with the natural outflow of team accountability. Rather than staff members and volunteers simply thinking of themselves as responsible to the senior pastor, they feel accountable to the entire team, as well.

To clarify this idea of the organization or church as person a bit more, how might this sound and feel in a team meeting? Let's say you are meeting with your team in a weekly setting and there are two items on the agenda: one, the church picnic that took place last week and two, the citywide community service project coming up next week. Accountability could work in at least two ways. Consider these two approaches to accountability:

Model #1: Pastor Accountability. In this scenario the pastor calls the meeting to order, opens in prayer, and tells the team that he is counting on them to do their jobs. How they do their jobs and carry out their roles is a reflection on him and his leadership. Among the questions he asks: "What was your particular assignment at the picnic?" "How do you feel you did?" "Did you do what I asked you to do?" "What are you going to do to make sure the community project next week goes the way I want it to go?" "What do you believe I am expecting from you?"

Model #2: Team Accountability. In this approach the pastor-team facilitator calls the team together and asks someone to open in prayer. Then he asks the team, "What items are most important for us to cover in this meeting? Which ones are most strategically important to the church?" The team members will likely acknowledge that the evaluation of last week's picnic and some time spent on more planning for the upcoming community outreach top the list. If other items are mentioned instead, the pastor-facilitator can then add the items he feels are needed and set an agenda for discussion. He also works to ensure that the team clarifies the goals of each of the discussions. He asks strategic questions. As events are evaluated and planned the questions include: "In order to reach our goal, what does the team needs from you?" or "If we hope to reach our goals, what changes does the team need you to make?"

In the first scenario, the team members are really not a team at all; they are merely reports to the pastor. This is a legitimate way to do work. Many churches and organizations still operate this way today. But the most effective ones do not! This is one way to accomplish your work, but it is certainly not a team. If this is the approach you are going to take, do yourself and your workers a favor and don't call it a team, just call it a staff meeting. To merely call your workers or volunteers a team will not make them into a team. It will only make them frustrated teaming wannabes!

A Team by Name Only?

Don't just call your group a team—treat them like one. One university leader, Del Chittim, told me,

I have seen a lot of pastors struggle with this. Particularly older leaders. They went to school at a time where you sat in rows, it was forbidden to let anyone see your work, and you basically learned how to not collaborate. Younger leaders, however, grew up in schools where your desks faced four other kids, you worked on team assignments, and shared homework assignments online. There is a lot of tension for young leaders in churches when older leaders are calling their staff a "team" and reading all the right books and using the right buzzwords in the interviews. Unfortunately after just three months of working, these young, talented guys are hitting the eject button.

Teamwork is just that—work! Don't get me wrong. When a team has hit its stride and is firing on all cylinders, when the team members are knit together and collaborative, that is an absolute joy. But, no team just gets there. A process is involved. Just ask any NFL coach on the tail end of a summer training camp. *Team* and *teaming* are more verbs than nouns!

Vital and vibrant church cultures are fueled by shared values. Part of the DNA of a great church and one made up of great teams is a strong sense of connection to a similar set of values. Simply put, values represent the principles and convictions that are most important to the ways in which a community determines to worship, relate, and live. Teaming values inform teaming leaders and the teaming churches they lead. These values are solidly biblical and practical. What, then, are the primary values of teaming churches and teaming leaders? To begin with, they require a solid commitment to developing deep trust on the team, to tolerating no elephants in the room, and to cultivating a strong sense of accountability to the team among the team members.

Tapping Team DNA

Team DNA represents the potential a team has for becoming; that is, for becoming together what they could never become individually. Joyfully, there are teams who work well together and come to realize their team DNA or their teaming potential, also known as their collective brilliance. However, there are also many teams who never truly tap their potential. They don't even come close. They skim the surface, tolerating shallow relationships, taunting elephants, and a lack of trust. One of the most frequent reasons this occurs is that they fail to identify clear and compelling goals. Although they may come together because of their faith or church roles, they fail to go anywhere together, because the team remains underchallenged.

What does it take to build a great team with great goals?

A Teaming Leader Interview, Medium-Sized Church: Murphy Matheny

*Murphy Matheny, pastor,
Cedar Lake Christian Assembly, Biloxi, Mississippi,
www.cedarlake.net*

Q: How long have you pastored this church?

A: Ten-and-a-half years

Q: What is your current average weekly attendance?

A: 625

Q: How important and integral are teams and teambuilding to your church? What role have they played throughout its history so far and what role do they play today?

A: Teams are vital to the health of the church because they provide the manpower to accomplish the processes in which day-to-day ministry takes place. Ongoing effective ministry is not likely apart from teams where (1) individuals can feel part of a bigger system that is accomplishing eternal purposes; (2) every person's gift can be fully utilized; and (3) work pressures are equalized among team members so that burnout is reduced or eliminated.

Q: What would you say makes for a great ministry team? What characterizes it?

A: (1) Communication—people usually do not function well if they feel "out of the loop." (2) Confidence—individual members know their gifts and feel confident in the areas where they are serving. (3) Core Values—every team member knows not only what to do, but why they are doing it. If teams are not on the same page concerning the "why," progress is slowed down or hindered.

Q: What does it take to turn a group of people into a real team? How can you tell when that happens?

A: (1) Clarification—it is necessary to clarify the vision and core values (with the team) so that no question remains about where the team is headed and what the expectations are. This should be done as a group so that the members have buy-in. (2) Attrition—when a team leader is unwavering in requiring commitment to a certain set of agreed upon values, not everyone in the group will join the team. This is an interesting point. Although the group may all agree to a set of values, when the implementation of those values begins to cut into traditional ways of thinking and acting, some will fall away because they either did not count the cost or they thought the team leader was not serious. (3) You know when you have a team when: (a) you begin to hear an echo of what you have been saying coming from the team members themselves; and (b) when they begin to naturally serve and help one another outside of their own areas of responsibility without being prompted to do so.

Q: What characterizes the most effective team players at your church? What does it take to be a great team player?

A: (1) They see beyond their area of responsibility to the big picture. (2) They are willing to serve for the good of the team regardless of recognition or remuneration. (3) They naturally recruit help for the leader's vision, not simply their own area. (4) They report to the team leader ideas or news from the field that will help the team effort. (5) They magnify and rely on the strengths of other team members, building them up with encouragement. What does it take? Humility.

Q: What are some essential practices and values of great team leaders?

A: (1) Integrity—the team leader must live the core values of the team before requiring the team members to live them as well. (2) Consistent communication—the leader needs to continuously discuss the vision with the team, celebrating victories, and correcting shortcomings. (3) Encouragement—great team leaders always encourage, in fact they believe that they cannot over-encourage. (4) Swift conflict resolution—conflict can either destroy the team or make it closer, depending on how it is handled. If it is allowed to go unaddressed for long periods of time, it becomes debilitating to team members who lose their excitement about their job. If it is handled swiftly and appropriately through biblical confrontation, it will often strengthen the relationships involved and reinforce biblical standards of respect and care in communication practices.

Q: What are some of the best questions you have ever asked your team?

A: Who is your mentor? Who are you mentoring right now? Do you trust me? Are you so busy putting out fires that you have no time to personally invest in those God has placed in your care?

Q: How important is a great goal to a great team?

A: It is extremely important because it focuses everyone's energy in one direction.

Drawing Your Circle

Questions to Ask Your Team

1. What makes for a great ministry team?
2. What does it take to increase the sense of trust on a team?
3. Do ministry teams tend to spot the elephant in the room soon enough? Explain.
4. How can a team develop more of a sense of mutual accountability for their ministry and areas of responsibility?
5. How candid are we with one another as a team?
6. When was the last candid moment we shared as a team? Was it awkward? Was it ultimately productive? How so?

Chapter Four

The Carrot: Teaming Motivation

*Teams are much more effective when they are
reaching toward goals that are impossible.*
—*Bobby Gruenewald, founder of YouVersion.com*

I remember the day I saw Moses cross the finish line—Moses *Tanui*, that is. It wasn't the Mt. Sinai Marathon, but the 100th running of the Boston Marathon. Before that year, typically about ten thousand people would sign on to run the most famous of all marathons on Patriot's Day in New England. Because of the significance of that centennial year, however, almost forty thousand had registered to run. Perhaps people wanted to tell their grandkids about the day they ran in the 100th Boston Marathon.

Although forty thousand people ran that day, forty thousand did not finish the race.

Not wanting to miss a piece of history in the city in which I served as a pastor, I took my family downtown and found a spot near the finish line to watch the historic results. Something surprising happened. As fun as it was watching the incredible Kenyan, Tanui, win the race that day and to see so many other runners who had trained so hard in Africa and had competed so well at this event, their runs were not the most dramatic. The ones that provided the most inspiration, and quite a bit of entertainment as well, were those who came in hours after the frontrunners.

As we sat on the cool April day, sipping on coffee and munching on slices of pizza, watching the results on the streets of Boston, we saw every kind of runner you can imagine. Two competitors had gotten married just before the start of the race. The groom ran clad in a tuxedo topcoat with shorts and the bride in a wedding gown with a short skirt and bridal white tennis shoes with real lace shoelaces.

That day in Boston, we saw it all. We saw people running dressed as clowns, necktied businessmen, Revolutionary soldiers, minutemen, firefighters, Batman, Robin, ballerinas, jugglers, Tarzan, King Kong, and all kinds of getups. An hour after the winners crossed the line, we began to see the middle-aged crew making their way, pushing hard to the finish line. The arrival of these competitors aroused a new round of cheers. One by one families, wives, children, and coworkers raised their voices, rooting on dads, granddads, moms, and grandmothers, stirring their souls on so that they could come in 29,231st, instead of simply settling for the 29,232nd place. The stakes were high, the symbolism poignant, and the emotions strong. One by one, we saw people accomplish their dream and reach their goal on the strength of willpower and a host of cheering and beloved encouragements.

God only knows the motivations that fueled the souls of the thousands of amateurs who had spent months training with one goal in mind: simply making it to the finish line of the Boston Marathon. Among them: the determination to lose weight, bounce back from a terrible illness, recover from a devastating job loss, accomplish something new with a friend or spouse or child, check another item off on their bucket list, or simply respond to a dare. Regardless of the reason, each runner had found a goal compelling enough to drive one foot ahead of the other for 26.22 miles, even as their tired limbs began to scale the terrain of Heartbreak Hill, the much-dreaded ascent that comes about twenty miles from the start of the race.

What is it that drives someone to engage in a marathon? What is the carrot, the motivation, or the reward? When runners reach the dreaded twentieth mile, what pushes them ahead to the twenty-first and twenty-second? That day at the Boston Marathon there was no shortage of personal drive, but there was also a mountain of encouragement from family, friends, and people on the team.

Consider these quotes from former marathoners:

> I've learned that finishing a marathon isn't just an athletic achievement. It's a state of mind; a state of mind that says anything is possible. —John Hanc, writer and runner

> Training for a marathon is an act of faith. Actually running the marathon is an act of courage. With faith and courage, ordinary humans can accomplish great things! —Randy Essex

65

Sometimes it's just surreal out there while you're running a marathon. People just standing out in the cold, even the rain, cheering for you, blasting music for you. It's an awesome show of camaraderie and community. —John Roberts

Focus, possibility, faith, courage, camaraderie, and community—these are the words of these souls who have done more than just talk about marathons. They have put their hearts and feet to running them. And you can hear the determinations of mind and heart and the strength of support that comes from those who cheer them on.

Going after the Prize—Paul, the Runner

Paul was apparently intrigued with running. He encouraged the Christ-followers in his day not only to run, but to run the race of life and to follow Christ with the will to win.

Don't you know that all the runners in the stadium run, but only one gets the prize? So run to win. Everyone who competes practices self-discipline in everything. The runners do this to get a crown of leaves that shrivel up and die, but *we do it to receive a crown* that never dies. So now *this is how I run—not without a clear goal in sight.* (1 Cor 9:24-26 CEB, italics mine)

Paul draws heavily on the metaphor and world of runners from the Greek tradition of the Olympics (that is, "in the stadium"). But he not only calls the follower of Christ to run, but to go hard after "the prize." All runners run with a compelling goal in mind; it fuels their journey and pushes them through the challenging places to the finish line. Paul says, "So now this is how I run—not without a clear goal in sight." In this instance in 1 Corinthians, Paul alludes to the ultimate prize of attaining everlasting life and the fulfillment of God's call. But, the truth is, not only do great runners need compelling goals to keep them focused and running, great teams also need great goals. In fact, many teams lose their fire and life because they either have no goal or what I call fuzzy goals.

The Power of the Prize

Many teams take too long trying to define and redefine their vision and not long enough determining clear and compelling goals. The vision is where you want to go, but the goals are the steps that will get you there. While the vision may be grand and vivid, the goals should be measured and clear. The vision is where you want to ultimately be. The goals are the steps and stop points that will get you to the vision.

How compelling would it be if every year on Patriot's Day in Boston if the poster simply read this way:

Patriot's Day in Boston
Come and run with us.

It might sound a bit preposterous, but some ministry team's goals feel exactly that way. They include function but no challenging measurable goals. They are fuzzy, at best. Fuzzy goals say, "We are going to have a children's church." Clear goals say, "We are going to have an exciting children's ministry that disciples fifty boys and girls this year and reaches twenty of their friends with the gospel of Christ." See the difference? One is vague and perfunctory; the other is compelling, clear, and challenging.

How about this marathon announcement instead?

The 117th Boston Marathon
26.3 miles
From Hopkinton, Massachusetts to Downtown Boston
First Place Wins: $100,000
April 17th
Starting Times:
9:00 A.M.: Mobility Impaired Program
9:17 A.M.: Push Rim Wheelchair Division
9:22 A.M.: Hand-cycle Participants
9:32 A.M.: Elite Women
10:00 A.M.: Elite Men and First Wave
10:20 A.M.: Second Wave
10:40 A.M.: Third Wave

Clarity and specificity can be compelling. Blurriness and uncertainty can slow a runner and a team down.

Fuzzy Goals?

One important question to ask your team and team members, and often, is: Are the goals of our team clear to you? And, in order to double check, add these questions: What is our next goal? Have we reached it yet? When will we reach our goal? How will you know when it is reached? How often do you remind your teams of their goals?

Most teams lag and languish because they have fuzzy goals. For a number of reasons, teams with fuzzy goals have lost their aim. They have moved from running the race to taking a vocational stroll in the park, like the singer Chuck Berry, with "no particular place to go."

What teams need to develop and constantly sharpen are SMART goals. What are the differences between fuzzy goals and SMART goals?

Fuzzy Goals Are …	SMART Goals Are …
Vague	Specific
Uncertain	Measurable
Unattainable	Attainable
Unrealistic	Realistic
Ill-timed	Timed and Timely

Here is a set of questions that SMART teams will ask themselves regularly about their goals:

- Is our goal **SPECIFIC** enough? What would make it even more specific?

- Is our goal really **MEASURABLE**? How could it be more clearly measurable?

- Is our goal truly **ATTAINABLE**? Is it challenging, but within reach?

- Do we have **REALISTIC** goals? Are they real world goals?

- Are our goals **TIMELY**? Is this what we need to be doing most at "such a time as this"?

There are motivational dynamics related to SMART or fuzzy goals. Teams not only need the extrinsic motivations of clear goals, they also need the intrinsic motivations that come from the right kind of goals. In your goal setting, consider this:

Fuzzy Goals Are …	SMART Goals Are …
Too Long	Concise
Forgettable	Memorable
Unexciting	Compelling

Every Team Needs a Carrot

While a true biblical team is a circle of honor, there is something else that is essential to forming a great team. Honor represents the character of the team and the relationships in which they share. Members of a true biblical team honor God and one another. They practice what Scot McKnight refers to as the Jesus Code: *"You must love the Lord your God with your whole heart, with your whole being, with your whole strength, and with your whole mind, and love your neighbor as yourself"* (Luke 10:27 CEB). It is an essential value. But, although honor creates the character of a team, honor alone will not move that team forward. That will also require a truly compelling goal. So, remember the Teaming Church Principle: "To become a great team your group must have *a deeply challenging goal*, a creatively empowering leader, and a collaborative, biblically honoring community."

Goal Tending and SWOT

Goals are found in two key areas of life—*opportunities* and *threats.* They are best faced and taken on by ministry teams dependent upon God, interdependent upon one another, and in touch with reality; that is, with their strengths and weaknesses.

A SWOT (Strength, Weaknesses, Opportunities, Threats) analysis, an approach to organizational evaluation developed at Stanford University in the 1960s, will help you and your team to evaluate the internal factors of your ministry—that is, the strengths and weaknesses. It will also help you consider the external factors—or the opportunities and threats.

The SWOT analysis, taken in a spirit of prayer and honesty, will help you as a team and as a leader to tap the best collective thinking of your entire team and to draw upon their insights. It will help create a seedbed of ideas for the right goals to set for your ministry. A SWOT analysis includes evaluating your organizations in the following areas and with the following types of questions:

- Strengths: What are your strengths as a team? As a church? As a team leader/member?

- Weaknesses: What are your weaknesses as a team? As a church? As a team leader/member?

- Opportunities: What are the opportunities your organization, church, or team are now facing? Where are potential effective areas of involvement?

- Threats: What are some of the things that threaten you as a team? As a church?

The Friendship of Crisis

Pastor and leadership specialist Sam Hemby claims we are living in a time when goals are no longer primarily determined by intentional efforts that are visionary and entrepreneurial. Many goals today are discovered (or born) in the midst of fire, in the heat of conflict and crisis.

In many ways the crises around us—global social, financial, and spiritual upheaval—is creating a list of clear and present goals for churches and church teams. A world in need presents a world of potential goals for churches and teams. In times past, we often found ourselves talking about teams and the organizational benefits of teams. In some places it was given merely token and periodic acclaim. Today, however, teams have become an organizational necessity. Hemby says, "The crises around us are making teams essential."

The idea of crisis as friend is a well-established theme in the Bible. James taught us to "count it all joy" when we fall into various struggles and crises, because they create agendas for God's help, provisions, and strength (cf. James 1:2). Peter talks about "fiery ordeals," "tests," and "sufferings" and says that when these come we should "rejoice" because they are the scenarios in which God's "glory" will be revealed (cf. 1 Pet 4:12-13).

In light of the SWOT analysis, remember your best team opportunities for setting goals are not only found amidst your organizational strengths and opportunities, but also in your threats and weaknesses. Jesus, in fact, renewed his compelling and incarnational goals as he looked a bit closer at the people to whom he had been sent and took a mental SWOT analysis of his own:

> Now when Jesus saw the crowds, he had compassion for them because they were troubled and helpless, like sheep without a shepherd. Then he said to his disciples, "The size of the harvest is bigger than you can imagine, but there are few workers. Therefore, plead with the Lord of the harvest to send out workers for his harvest."

> He called his twelve disciples and gave them authority over unclean spirits to throw them out and to heal every disease and every sickness. (Matt 9:36–10:1 CEB)

Just look at the Master Teaming Leader at work: in this setting, Jesus embraced the friendship of crisis. He saw the threats: "they were troubled and helpless." He saw their weaknesses: "they were . . . like sheep without a shepherd." And, he decided it needed a team response: "He called his twelve disciples and gave them authority." And, he gave that team compelling goals: "to heal every disease and every sickness."

Team Meetings—Just Two Things!

Team meetings are a necessity, but they don't have to be long and laborious. On the contrary, they can be interesting, encouraging, and even exciting, if they stay on focus. Actually, the only two things that need to be done in effective regular team meetings are community building and goal tending. Community building represents all the things a team does to keep current on one another's lives and experiences and to stay connected interpersonally. This includes learning more about your team members' families, their personal goals and achievements, their hobbies, their interests, their joys and their struggles; showing interest in their hearts and lives; and praying for one another. While a team meeting generally is not a place to go into great depth in these areas, it is important that the team stay up-to-date with key personal information. This reminds us that we are not just a ministry team or a group of people working on a project—we are a community of people, of Christ-followers with real lives and real issues.

Here are a few great questions for community building on your team:

Great Community-Building Team Questions

- What are some challenges you are facing personally?
- How can we pray for you and your family?
- What is one of your greatest joys recently?
- What is one of your greatest disappointments recently?

Goal tending represents all of the practices and exercises a good team does to determine, set, measure, monitor, and reach their ministry goals. This includes taking regular SWOT analyses, blue sky dreaming, brainstorming sessions, goal setting, activity and project evaluations, making sure your goals stay clear and buoyant (and not fuzzy), celebrating goals achieved as a team, and praying for God's direction in your shared ministry.

In the next chapter we will look at the stages that turn ministry groups into teams; there are four of them. But, for now, here are a few great questions for goal tending on your team:

Great Goal-Tending Team Questions

- If you (or your ministry team) could do anything you wanted to do to serve God's purposes and be guaranteed it would succeed, what would you do?

- How will you know when you have reached your goals?
- What currently is working against you reaching your goals?
- What currently is helping you reach your goals?

Drawing Your Circle

Questions to Ask Your Team

1. Has anyone ever run in a marathon? What did the experience teach you? What did it require of you?

2. Are your team goals fuzzy or SMART? Explain.

3. What would it take to make your team goals SMART-er?

4. Can a crisis be a friend to a team? To a church? How so?

5. Describe the ideal productive team meeting. What would it look like? What would it include? Do your meetings qualify? If not, what changes would make them more effective?

6. What is the most challenging goal your team is currently taking on?

Once Upon a Team— Scene Three

The Second Donut

"So, tell me about this dream team in your church," Glenn insisted, dipping the second donut into a fresh cup of coffee. "How many are on the team?"

"Only seven."

"Seven is a good size team," Glenn said.

"What is the ideal size, in your opinion?"

Glenn laughed. "Guess how Jeff Bezos, the founder of Amazon.com, answered that question in a recent interview for *Fast Company* magazine?"

"I have no idea."

"The number of people it takes to eat one large pizza . . . about five or six."

"Ha. He doesn't know how much pizza I can polish off just by myself!" Scott added, laughing too.

"You and me too! But, seriously, from my experience I would say six to twelve is an ideal size for a team," Glenn added. "Any more than that and the teaming dynamics begin to break down; only a few voices are heard. But, let me hear more about your best team."

"Yes. The seniors group. What a phenomenal group of people, or, I should say, team. Well, it all goes back to a great older couple who had been members of our church for more than fifteen years, Arthur and Lucille.

You talk about two people who just gave of themselves and rarely asked for anything in return. 'Selfless' definitely describes who they were."

"Were?"

"Well, yes, a couple of years ago, Lucille was diagnosed with cancer and within a short number of months passed away, leaving Arthur to take care of himself. Arthur was in his mideighties and starting to get quite feeble—a strong spirit though, and a sharp mind, but an uncooperative body."

"Did he own a home?"

"Yes, that's a big part of this team story. You see, Arthur and Lucille had lived in the same house for more than fifty years. Lucille having been such a loving caregiver to Arthur before she passed away, we were all convinced that Arthur would have to go to a rest home, even though it was the last thing he wanted to do."

"How did he handle it?"

"Well, I had a very interesting visit from Jean, a member of the church who was a friend of Arthur and Lucille. She was in her sixties at the time, quite vibrant and active in the church. She had a question for me the morning she arrived at my office.

"Jean told me how sad she and the other five or six members of their small group were over the loss of Lucille and how concerned they all were about Arthur's future. They were all dreading seeing him have to move out of his house and away from their small group.

"I responded, 'It's so sad and it appears that Arthur is going to have to move out of his home. He is just too feeble to be at home by himself all day.'

"Jean nodded her head and said, 'Yes, Pastor, we know. We are all so concerned, but I have to tell you something. We have been praying, thinking, and talking as a group and we have an idea we want to run by you.'

"'Certainly.' I said, 'What's the idea?'

"'Well,' she said, 'most of us on the team are in our sixties and employed part-time, but we believe we can help Arthur stay in his home.'

"So I said, 'That will take quite a bit of money. I understand how much all of you care, but this is a huge task. But how will you do this, by taking up an offering? Are you going to hire someone?'

"She said, 'No, Pastor, we would like to offer our services to Arthur. You see, because of our varied schedules—we think we have an idea worked out that will help. One of us can come by Arthur's house in the morning on our way to work and make sure he is out of bed and that he eats some breakfast. Then, another one of us can come by around midday each day, tidy up the house a bit, make lunch, and enjoy some conversation with Arthur. Then, out of the four couples in our group, we can rotate bringing dinner over to Arthur each evening.'

"I said, 'You would be willing do that?'

"She said, 'Well, that's why I am here today, Pastor.'

"'I'm not sure I understand,' I said.

"'I am here to ask your permission,' Jean said, 'for us to do this for Arthur. Is it okay with you? Do you think this is something the Lord and the church would approve of?'

"Can you imagine, Glenn? She wanted to know if God would approve of it."

"Sounds like someone who respects her pastor's view and opinion," Glenn said.

"As you can imagine, I looked at her and said, 'Of course I think God would approve of it. In fact, it sounds just like something Jesus would do. Truthfully, I think the idea is absolutely beautiful. But, let me ask you. Have you worked out the details, counted the personal cost of this, and do you think it is something all of you can commit to over an extended period?'

"She said yes, and then she said, 'We all met at my home last night and spent about three hours working through all of the details. We wrote up a full schedule. We have just a couple of loose ends to tie down, but it appears to be coming together well. So, do we have your approval?'

"I said, 'You have my glowing approval and, not only that, you have my deep appreciation. And, Jean, you have made this pastor proud.'"

"How's their plan working so far?" Glenn asked.

"Like a charm. Their sense of joy and community has never been stronger. And Arthur seems to appreciate what they are doing so much."

Shaking his head and smiling, Glenn said, "That is one of the most beautiful team stories I have ever heard, Scott. Wow. Talk about experiencing a new kind of community in Christ! Talk about a circle of honor. That's great."

"You know, I thought the same thing, Glenn. It really is a powerful example of authentic community."

"And just think of it, Scott. What is God using to turn that small group into a true team?" Glenn couldn't miss the opportunity to offer another insight.

"Arthur's loss?" Scott said.

"Yes, through a conflict or the awareness of a difficult problem. Arthur's great need is becoming a great goal over that great group of people and that has built one great team. More than anything, it is bringing great glory to God."

"Can you say that again?" Scott asked as he picked up his cell phone and typed. "I want to write that last sentence down."

"Sure. And while you are doing so, you know what else just hit me?"

"No, what's that?" Scott asked.

"Can you imagine being a part of a community with a better 'social security' program than that?"

"Ha. I never thought of it that way! Man, I wish some of that attitude and community could spill over on others, starting with the worship leader. But, it won't take care of it all. I know the problem is bigger than one person."

"How much bigger?"

"Well, I think that the worship leader is probably just one of maybe ten or twelve key influencers in the church who have similar mind-sets," Scott said.

"And what type of 'mind-set' is that, a boss mind-set or a controlling mind-set?"

"Either of those fits like a glove."

"Let me ask you another question, Scott."

"Sure. You seem to know the right ones to ask."

"Does it feel like the church is moving forward or falling behind?"

"Wow. That is a tough one to answer. Honestly, our numbers do both. It seems that one month we will creep ahead in attendance and giving, only to be followed by another month where we see a downturn. Most of the time I don't know whether to be hopeful or concerned," Scott said.

"So, you say the church feels . . . 'stuck,' " Glenn started the sentence and paused, hoping Scott would finish it.

"Absolutely, we really do. We are neither failing miserably nor advancing steadily. We are sort of languishing."

"How would you describe the mood or attitude of the congregation in general?"

"Honestly, what my gut tells me is that about half of them are content to see the church remain as it is and the other half is bored."

"So, the question about the worship leader is not the only one on your mind today. What's the biggest question you are living with as a pastor?"

"That's easy. What do you do when your church feels stuck?"

"Well," Glenn said, "unfortunately the hour I blocked for our coffee meeting is almost up."

"Oh, sorry, Glenn. I am probably talking your ear off."

"No. This is important stuff and I appreciate you confiding in me, Scott. I tell you what, let me just give my wife a quick call and let her know I will be home a little later than I thought."

"Are you sure? You probably have more important things to tend to."

"You're right. And today, that 'important thing' is right here talking with you."

Scott smiled and headed back to the counter for a warm-up. He felt encouraged and somehow more secure just to be meeting with this seasoned leader.

Glenn pulled out his cell phone and dialed home.

Scott offered up a silent thank you to God for a newfound friend and confidant; possibly the mentor he had been praying for.

Part Two

Teach Your Team to Draw Circles— The Teaming Technique

Building a great church involves not just drawing circles, but developing a team of circle drawers. As long as a leader is willing to build a team of leaders (that is, circle drawers) the potential of the team is maximized and the potential for growth in the church is in the hands of God.

Chapter Five

Turning Groups into Teams

The team remains the most flexible and the most powerful unit of performance, learning, and change in any organization.
—*Jon R. Katzenbach and Douglas K. Smith*

When you're a part of a team, you need to have a common vision. That's the problem that most teams face, that everyone isn't on the same page. You all need to understand what you're striving for.
—*Don Felder, former guitarist, The Eagles*

If a church is like a person, then sometimes churches get tired, discouraged, even lazy, or stuck. In our lives, psychologically and spiritually, we experience peaks of high performance and opportunity and valleys of uncertainty and discouragement. The cycles that local churches go through are often quite similar to the patterns people face because churches are comprised of people.

But just how frustrated do people, or churches for that matter, have to become before they change? John Maxwell has said it well: "People change when they hurt enough that they *have* to, learn enough that they *want* to, or receive enough that they are *able* to."[1]

Frustrated with their own ineffectiveness and with their shrinking congregations amidst a thriving business community, a group of Anglican leaders was determined to make some efforts toward change. They appointed a council made up of clergy and business leaders to take a hard and honest look at the state of their churches. Their report acknowledged that "it is a socially fluid society to which . . . inflexible church organizations fashioned for more stable times, [have] adapted itself. The church's life has been slow to take [this] into account and meet the complex needs of [a] changing society."[2]

Socially fluid society? Inflexible church? Slow church? Does this sound familiar?

The Paul Report Council was primarily designed in order for clergy to ask believing business leaders what changes they saw that the church needed to make in order to be more effective. Before suggestions were made, however, the clergy leaders had to hear some honest critique. The final results of the report determined that this particular denomination had misread its culture and its moment within that culture as well as its responsibility to that culture. As a result, the report was full of truthful, confrontational, and hard-to-hear, but much-needed, insights including these that strike a fresh chord today:

> The Church today has to be able to . . . retain its dynamic and refuse to be ossified; it needs fluidity, mobility, flexibility. It's not a [cozy] club. It exists entirely for those who are not its members. But what happens? A new area springs up. The Church begins to meet in one another's homes. They begin to go out caring for the community. But all too soon their thoughts turn towards a church building. They burden themselves with a vast church and church hall, a debt . . . , and maintenance problems—and immediately become turned in on themselves; servants of the "Static Church," they're a [cozy] club, not a caring community; they're no longer geared to mission but maintenance.[3]
>
> The old [approaches to church life, preferred by older generations] has to be allowed to live, and the new has to be allowed to grow alongside of it. The most important thing is to create new forms of ministry to introduce into areas where the old. . . . system has broken down.[4]
>
> We believe the Church is hording vast reserves of service which can be mobilized if our people are specifically asked what they can do and are directed to the jobs.[5]

What a scathing indictment for the church of that day this report must have been: "the Church is hording vast reserves of service."

What an accurate read on the nature of a church once it becomes self-consumed and stuck: "they're a cozy club, not a caring community; they're no longer geared to mission but maintenance."

What a spot-on observation of the need of the hour for the church that is stuck: "the most important thing is to create new forms of ministry to introduce into areas where the old . . . system has broken down."

The Paul Report describes an Anglican church struck in the 1960s and many of today's churches as well. Some have said that the church in Europe is a portent of the church in America. This is an insight worth considering. As I read through the assortment of books that sprang from this report compiled in the 1960s, it seemed many were freshly published and describing today's church. We can take a cue from history.

> What has been is what will be,
>> and what has been done is what will be done;
>> and there is nothing new under the sun. (Eccl 1:9 ESV)

Three Team Illnesses

The church is only as strong as the teams of which it is comprised. Similarly, the wise pastor who wants to see her church revitalized must invest herself in revitalizing or rebuilding the teams that make up that church. In essence, to improve the larger circle, the smaller ones must first be tended to.

Although the apostle Paul enjoyed amazing opportunities to plant new churches and develop existing ones, he also constantly dealt with church conflicts and dysfunction. Clearly Paul's method of developing congregations and facing their conflicts comes back to his role as a ministry team leader. His answer to the problems wasn't wringing his hands or even simply praying about the problems (as important as that is); Paul, instead, rolled up his sleeves and appointed teams and team members to engage the conflicts. His letters directed and inspired them to deal with opportunities and threats head on in the love and wisdom of Christ.

I see at least three illnesses that develop on ministry teams and teams of every kind today: team freeze, team lock, and team rust. Let's take a brief look at each and how to avoid these slow-downs in your church and on your team.

Team Freeze

This occurs when teams develop (sometimes through lack of leadership) a certain relational distance. Sometimes work groups in churches can get so focused on tasks or titles that they easily forget to value the people with whom they serve. Warmth exits the team, motivation diminishes or changes, honor is overlooked, and there is a certain chill in the air. The team undergoing team freeze has lost its sense of connectedness and warmth.

There are ways to deal with and to avoid team freeze. Leading teams requires a certain level of emotional intelligence. Granted, some people are born with large doses of it; others of us have to work hard to develop it. There are times on a team where the team leader needs to look into the faces of his team members and say, "Let's just put the agenda aside for a while. Let's take some time to focus on one another." Remember, one of the most important aspects of a ministry team is that members are regularly sharing in and experiencing community together. If you don't experience it together, it is awfully difficult to reproduce in other areas.

Your ministry is not just about what you do together, but who you are and what you share together as a team. Remember, as a team, you are not only working and serving—you are also becoming. That's what people will notice the most; not just what the team does, but how the team interacts with one another. Be the team that others want to emulate.

Team Lock

This is a condition that develops when teams face unresolved issues. The problem occurs when a team leader either doesn't see the issue (that is, the elephant in the room) or sees it and chooses not to address it. Unresolved issues on a team diminish open environments and tend to shut down collaboration among team members. As we dig in our heels, we hinder the fluidity, the flow, and the nimbleness of the team. Minds close and work slows.

Avoidance becomes kryptonite. The unspoken tensions on a team do not disappear when left unaddressed, they just intensify. When obvious elephants are ignored, team members first become confused and, eventually, even angry, resenting the fact that the team leader is choosing to overlook more obvious issues. We become more determined to prove ourselves right than to be in right relationship with our team and team members.

There are different ways to open up a group experiencing team lock. The best way, however, is to work hard at creating and maintaining an open and honest culture. Although it may be awkward at first, acknowledge the elephant or elephants in the room and work hard to hunt them down. It's time for an organizational safari! Remember, a tedious peace is no peace at all. It is better for a team to talk through, work through, and pray through conflict than work at holding up a house of peace cards. Honesty is still the best policy—on teams and everywhere else. Remember, for team health and strength, candor rules!

Team Rust

When goals get old and remain unreached, unmeasured, or undefined, the team can feel worn, weary, and sluggish. Rust tends to set in when church systems are no longer measured, honestly examined, and refreshed.

Unfortunately, church members sometimes want to see innovation and new ideas in government, in their companies, in their communities, but not in their church. It is tempting to turn our worn systems and volunteer groups into sacred icons to hold on to. The familiarity of having one place in our life that never changes can sometimes be comforting, falsely so; but if we allow the church to take on such a pattern or to maintain the same, it is the lost that suffer.

Keep the cogs, wheels, and gears on your team moving briskly by keeping your team challenged. Being on a team should bring a certain sense of comfort or encouragement to the team members. However, comfort alone becomes the enemy of a team. Great teams regularly experience the comfort of community, but also the challenge of collaboration, compelling goals, and even conflicts. It is the balance of grace and truth. Somehow, they rest and they run, regularly. In fact, if they rest without running, they will ossify. And, if they just run without resting, they will grow tired and unfocused. Teams are best challenged by having clear goals, frequent measurements of those goals, celebrations of goals achieved, and engaging questions that keep them on their toes, focused on their goals, and effective.

Four Stages of Team Development: The Tuckman Model

Bruce Tuckman wrote a book about the Boston Marathon called *The Long Road to Boston*. But, he is best known for outlining an even more important race, that of turning a group into a team. Tuckman was the author of a groundbreaking article published in 1965, titled "Developmental Sequence in Small Groups."[6] This piece has provided great insight to leaders of all types and in all disciplines on the vital work of turning a group into a team. His insights are unparalleled and invaluable in understanding the teaming process. In this section I lend a few new descriptive terms to the metaphorical process of running a race: start-up, breaking down, pacing, and stride. Here are the four stages, plus a fifth. If you are on a team currently or leading a team, your team is in one of these stages right now.

FORMING—The Start-Up of the Team

STORMING—The Breaking Down of the Team

NORMING—The Pacing of the Team

PERFORMING—The Team Finding Its Stride

Each of these four stages, and a potential fifth one, represent the development points in the life of a team. *Forming* is the birth of the team; *storming* is the adolescent stage; *norming* represents the early adulthood; and *performing* the prime and most productive period of a mature team's life.

Let's take a look at each of these stages and consider what is going on in the mind of the team members at each one. Also, we will emphasize the way a team leader should lead (or serve) a team at each of these important stages. The material on these next few pages is sort of a playbook for building your team, a map for becoming a truly great and high performing ministry. You will want to refer to it often.

Stage One: The Start-Up (Forming)

start up [stahrt-uhp]	(*noun*) the act or fact of starting something; a setting in motion.

In a race, runners have to set their feet into the starting blocks. They have to find their places and prepare to run. As a team is brought together for the first time, Tuckman says that they are "unconscious and unskilled." That is a polite and technical way to say "they just don't know how bad they really are," or put a bit more positively, they don't know how much they yet have to learn about working together as a team.

Because of the basic naiveté that each member brings to the start of a new team, there is a certain set of questions they are generally asking. Among them: What is the purpose of the team? What specific role do I need to fill and how is it different from the other team members'? What is expected on the team and of the team? How much input should I give? Do I only answer questions asked by the team leader, or is it okay to ask some of my own?

The primary focus from the team leader at this starting point is structure—helping the team to take form. This involves a focus on helping the team determine its goal or goals clearly and concisely. It also requires much communication and help for each of the team members to understand their part to play in achieving these team goals. It includes discussions and training on not just how to work, but how to work together.

At this point, it is vital for the team leader to focus on helping the team set its course and direction. This involves communicating expectations and guidelines. Also, checking on the team's progress frequently, both in and out of meetings, is vital.

Stage Two: The Breaking Down (Storming)

break·down [breyk—doun]	(*noun*) a breaking down, wearing out, or sudden loss of ability to function efficiently, as of a machine.

One of my favorite television programs is a reality show called *Hard Knocks*. It chronicles the process of various team training camps in the NFL. It is fascinating to watch about sixty or seventy players practice in the heat of summer and fight their way onto a place on the team that by the beginning of the regular season must be whittled down to no more than fifty-three players. Typically a wide range of personalities show up among the rookie players, many of them feeling pretty cocky about the shot they have with the big boys. In no time, however, the pressure and strain of working with a team begins to break them down physically and psychologically. Chips on shoulders are dealt hard and swift blows at an NFL camp. It is an interesting process to watch unfold.

All teams, including church teams, go through this storming period. A closer look at Jesus' work with his own disciples reveals that he faced an intense period of storming in the process of getting his team into shape. Just think of it—the headstrong determinations of Peter, the doubts of Thomas, the demands of James and John's mother, the worries of Martha, and the fears of Mary, her sister. Before teams find their pace, they usually endure a conflict or two. This becomes a bit of the fire that burns the competitive egos out of team players' systems and helps them begin to feel the strength of not just working, but working together.

At the breaking down or storming stage, though difficult, the team is actually making progress. Tuckman says that at this point they are "conscious and unskilled." In other words, by now they know just how poorly prepared to be a team member they truly are. They find themselves in a weakened position and eventually in a place where they are willing to learn together. At this point the team members feel the need to express their concerns, their points of view, and their individuality. For the most part, the team leader needs to let them do so, to let them get it out of their systems, so to speak. This season involves some conflicts and the conflicts become the teachable moments.

It is important to remember that the enemy of teams is also the enemy of biblical community, and spiritual growth itself, for that matter. It is selfishness. Some of God's sovereign remedies for the pandemic disease of selfishness include marriage, family, community, ministry, and teams. While we have a tendency to focus on a team as simply a way to get a job done, remember the ultimate job is the one the Holy Spirit is doing in you and me. He is working "in [us] both to will and to do of his good pleasure" (Phil 2:13 KJV). And, just what is his "good pleasure"? That is conforming us into the image of Christ. Teams help to do that, but not without periodic tensions and conflicts.

The role the leader needs to play in the breaking down stage is that of coach. As the team and team members wrestle with their newfound awareness of just how much they don't know about working as a team, the leader needs to bring words of encouragement, belief, focus, and inspiration that "we will get through this stage and will find our pace as a team and team members quite soon."

Stage Three: The Pacing (Norming)

pac·ing [peys eng]	(*noun*) rate of movement, especially in stepping, walking, etc.

By stage three your group members start to find a rhythm in their roles and relationships. Tuckman says that at this point they are "conscious and skilled." In other words, they now know just how much improved they are becoming at working as a team. They can feel the changes in their roles and relationships. Things are beginning to gel. Collaborations have begun. Community is happening. They are turning from a group into a team. And, God is smiling on the process.

At this point in the team's development, as pacing occurs, the team members have begun to accept their respective roles, goals, and guidelines. They are connecting more with the processes, the systems, and procedures of their particular team. They are feeling the stimulation and challenge of clear and compelling goals. Their decisions more and more are being reached by consensus. They are beginning to fly as one.

The team leader at this stage is functioning more and more as a facilitator. After all, the team members are starting to pick up and play their instruments, and the leader is starting to simply conduct the music they are making together. The team leader is finding that leading by facilitating involves a few key practices:

- Asking helpful, valuable, and strategic questions;
- Helping team members develop their abilities and skills;

- Involving team members in decisions;

- Holding frequent and focused team meetings and gatherings;

- Listening to the team members' problems and concerns;

- Helping team members frame issues and engage conflicts effectively;

- Recognizing positive outcomes; and

- Acknowledging team spirit and the achievement of goals.

Stage Four: The Stride (Performing)

stride [strahyd]	(*idiom*) to reach the point or level at which one functions most competently and consistently: i.e., the quarterback didn't hit his stride until the second half of the game.

The ultimate stage to which every team should aspire is that of the stride. This is the place at which a team becomes a high performance team; they really start to produce in life, community, service, and action. Unfortunately, because of a lack of focus, commitment, and true team leadership, many (and, more likely, most) teams never reach this level.

Tuckman says at the performing stage the team members are "unconscious and skilled." I actually interpret that as meaning they don't know how good they are! That is a great place to be—incredibly effective and genuinely humble. What an environment in which to serve! At this level, the team members have the right stuff and the right spirit—a winning combination. Capable and humble; who wouldn't love to have a team full of people like that? With prayer, patience, and commitment, it is entirely possible.

When teams hit their stride, the team members are no longer pretending. They reveal their true selves. In this kind of team environment, they are free to not only be at their best but also to offer their best. The open, honest, and honoring environment they enjoy minimizes their struggles with individual wants and wishes, as well as with ego overall. They by now have come to value and enjoy a team identity and a great team spirit. The team at this point is functioning with a real sense of biblical community. The Spirit of God is weaving lives together and creating a unified team. The circle is alive with the presence and blessing of God.

Stage Five: The Finish Line (Adjourning)

finish line [fi-nish līn]	(*noun*) a line marking the end of a race.

In 1977, Tuckman proposed a fifth stage to his popular model. After observing the ongoing research that his paper had engendered, he was encouraged to consider another stage that sometimes occurs in the process, called "adjourning." Adjourning is what occurs when a team is disbanded for any one of a number of reasons. In a fully functional scenario this would occur when a project team, for instance, has realized its goals. At that point, whether in a church or business, the temptation is to continue meeting as a team for the sake of relationship. While relationship, in particular in light of Christian fellowship, is vital, their ongoing function as a team may likely be impeded once the presence of a compelling goal is removed.

Churches tend to do a good job of starting things, but not such good a job of ending them. Pastors and team leaders need to be keenly aware when the environment calls for a new team to start up, but also when it is time to celebrate the accomplishments of a particular team and to conclude or adjourn. This affords the opportunity to form the next team or teams that the church most needs to grow and develop.

A few years ago, I asked our church elders to meet with each of the various ministry teams to help them evaluate their effectiveness and their needs. One of the teams was the Diaspora Team, a group of congregants from various parts of the world. The goal of this ministry had been to bring internationals in the church together to strengthen fellowship and to help them connect more fully within the community life of the church.

When the elder I appointed to this particular group met with the Diaspora Team for their evaluation, he eventually came to an important question: "What is your goal as a team?" At that point the team leader repeated, almost verbatim, what I wrote above. After stating the goal, the elder asked one more important question: "Have you achieved the goal?" The answer was a surprise.

"Yes. I believe we have."

As the room got quiet, one more question came: "Are there any other goals the church needs you to achieve on this team?"

"Come to think of it, no. In fact, the church has become so integrated that to continue to hold separate events for 'diaspora' people within the church would only preclude them from further integration into the church family."

At that meeting, the decision was made to shut down the Diaspora Team. Although it felt a little weird at first to shut down anything in the church, it proved to be the best thing we could have done. In the case of this team it was truly a case of mission accomplished. The best thing to do for ministry development at this point was not to start a new team, but to bring one to an honorable and timely end.

There are hundreds of beautiful and vital tasks of ministry, of serving the life and soul needs of the world in which God has placed us, just waiting to be carried out. The best way I know how to do so is through effective teams and teaming efforts. Not only are teams capable of getting much done in a short period of time, as they do so their unified efforts reflect something of Jesus, of his team of disciples, and of the glory of God

Moving people from their individualized lives and experiences into a teaming circle is a process. Getting them from the start-up, through the breaking down and into a stride of effective ministry will not be without some challenges. This will not only call for leadership; it will also call for a new kind of leader—a teaming leader.

Drawing Your Circle

Questions to Ask Your Team

1. Does your church or team ever feel stuck? How so?

2. What was one of the best teams you have ever been a part of? What made it so special?

3. Has your team ever caught one of the three team illnesses—team freeze, team lock, or team rust? Explain.

4. Which stage of development would you say your team is in? Start-up? Breakdown? Pacing? Stride? How can you tell?

5. What will it take for your team to get to the next stage of development? What will it require of you?

6. What kind of leader does it take to help a team become a truly great team?

Chapter Six

Teaming Leadership

Finding good players is easy.
Getting them to play as a team is another story.
—*Casey Stengel*

Teams are real messy at times because you have
to influence and persuade; you can't dictate.
—*Jim Mellado, president, Willow Creek Association*

Moses is the best example we have in the Bible of how to lead and how not to lead a team. In short, looking at his leadership journey, when God first called Moses to lead, he tried desperately to back out. Then, when he led the nation of Israel through the wilderness, he tried to do it on his own. But, after listening to a much-needed leadership lesson from his father-in-law, Jethro, he was transformed into a true teaming leader.

The premier biblical passage on the art of delegation, an essential team-building skill, is Exodus 18. At his breaking point, Moses, encumbered with the overwhelming responsibilities of leading the Hebrew children out of Egypt and toward the Promised Land, was visited by Jethro. After observing the struggles of Moses and his antiquated organizational style, he offered some fatherly (or father-in-lawly) advice. Here's the story:

> The next day, Moses took his seat to hear the people's disputes against each other. They waited before him from morning till evening.

When Moses' father-in-law saw all that Moses was doing for the people, he asked, "What are you really accomplishing here? Why are you trying to do all this alone while everyone stands around you from morning till evening?"

Moses replied, "Because the people come to me to get a ruling from God. When a dispute arises, they come to me, and I am the one who settles the case between the quarreling parties. I inform the people of God's decrees and give them his instructions."

"This is not good!" Moses' father-in-law exclaimed. "You're going to wear yourself out—and the people, too. This job is too heavy a burden for you to handle all by yourself. Now listen to me, and let me give you a word of advice, and may God be with you. You should continue to be the people's representative before God, bringing their disputes to him. Teach them God's decrees, and give them his instructions. Show them how to conduct their lives. But select from all the people some capable, honest men who fear God and hate bribes. Appoint them as leaders over groups of one thousand, one hundred, fifty, and ten. They should always be available to solve the people's common disputes, but have them bring the major cases to you. Let the leaders decide the smaller matters themselves. They will help you carry the load, making the task easier for you. If you follow this advice, and if God commands you to do so, then you will be able to endure the pressures, and all these people will go home in peace."(Exod 18:13-23 NLT)

After following Jethro's advice, instead of judging matters and disputes as the lone arbiter, Moses selected and brought together a team of judges. This made "the task easier" and lightened his workload. As a result, the people were served and matters resolved more effectively and Moses was probably prevented from a heart attack or some other breakdown. The man who would lead the Hebrew nation toward the promises, and the Promised Land, of God was becoming a teaming leader.

You've Got a Problem? I've Got a Team!

Later on in the wilderness journey, after a time of considerable complaining to Moses among the Hebrew children, it was apparently time for some changes to be made. Moses was feeling the pressure. For some time, the people had been eating manna (the heaven-sent food) God had provided and yet they were still craving meat. This not only frustrated Moses, it also angered God.

Moses heard all the families standing in the doorways of their tents whining, and the LORD became extremely angry.

Moses was also very aggravated. And Moses said to the LORD, "Why are you treating me, your servant, so harshly? Have mercy on me! What did I do to deserve the burden of all these people? Did I give birth to them? Did I bring them into the world? Why did you tell me to carry them in my arms like a mother carries a nursing baby? How can I carry them to the land you swore to give their ancestors? Where am I supposed to get meat for all these people? They keep whining to me saying, 'Give us meat to eat!' I can't carry all these people by myself! The load is far too heavy! If this is how you intend to treat me, just go ahead and kill me. Do me a favor and spare me this misery!" (Num 11:10-15 NLT)

Moses' complaints are reminiscent of Jethro's earlier observations and advice in Exodus 18. Clearly, Moses is now feeling alone and isolated in his responsibilities as a leader.

But, God had a remedy. It was time for a new team.

Then the LORD said to Moses, "Gather before me seventy men who are recognized as elders and leaders of Israel. Bring them to the Tabernacle to stand there with you. I will come down and talk to you there. I will take some of the Spirit that is upon you, and I will put the Spirit upon them also. They will bear the burden of the people along with you, so you will not have to carry it alone. (Num 11:16-17 NLT)

In this instance, God relieved the overwhelmed leader, Moses, not by taking away the people, nor by taking away his responsibility. The remedy did not come by sending him away on a sabbatical, or by disassociating him from them, or even by taking his life, as Moses actually requested. Instead, God relieved Moses by giving him something else—a new Spirit-anointed team, some seventy strong. It reminds me of the power and potential John Wesley recognized in a God-honoring team:

Give me one hundred men who fear nothing but sin and desire nothing but God, and I care not a straw whether they be clergyman or laymen, with them I will shake the gates of Hell and set up the kingdom of Heaven upon the earth.[1]

After voicing some doubts to God and receiving a word of correction (cf. Num 11:18-23), Moses implemented the new plan and selected a new team.

So Moses went out and reported the LORD's words to the people. He gathered the seventy leaders and stationed them around the Tabernacle. And the LORD came down in the cloud and spoke to Moses. Then he gave the seventy elders the same Spirit that was upon

Moses. And when the Spirit rested upon them, they prophesied. (Num 11:24-25 NLT)

Not only was a team raised up to assist Moses, for at least a time they acted very much like him, apparently emulating his example and God-given functions—full of the Spirit, preaching, prophesying, and being used of God. Joshua, the personal assistant to Moses, was alarmed by this behavior since he was accustomed to a more hierarchical leadership structure and saw these functions as the sole responsibility and privilege of Moses, the man of God. Used to being led by one man in a hierarchical environment, Joshua found the empowered team of leaders something apparently entirely new. He was clearly uncomfortable with the change. He said to his leader, "Eldad and Medad are prophesying in the camp! . . . Moses, my master, make them stop!" (Num 11:27-28 NLT).

Moses, however, responded quite differently to the implementation of a new team than did his assistant, Joshua. He had a different view of the event. Apparently Moses had already had his fill of solo leadership efforts and the burdens associated with it. He was exhausted and actually welcomed the emergence of a new team. This marked a significant moment in Israel's history and not only foreshadowed the Day of Pentecost, it represents the first account in Scripture of a Spirit-anointed team. You can hear in the wish or desire of Moses a change of heart. He had come to realize the value of not lording over others or simply using hierarchical tactics as a leader. He had come to value the power of a great team. Moses was learning how to draw circles.

But Moses replied [to Joshua], "Are you jealous for my sake? I wish that all the LORD's people were prophets, and that the LORD would put his Spirit upon them all!" Then Moses returned to the camp with the elders of Israel. (Num 11:29-30 NLT)

A little older and a little wiser, Moses saw something he had earlier missed. He had come to see so clearly that many hands made the task lighter and the effectiveness much greater. Teams don't add to your effectiveness as a leader, they multiply it.

The Teaming Church Principle #3: An Empowering Leader

Great teaming leaders are gifted and skilled to tap into the strengths and potentials of the individuals on the team, but more so of the team itself. The true teaming leader is a coach, and every great team needs one. They don't just need a leader, they need the right kind of leader. It is teaming

essential #3: "To become a great team your group must have a deeply challenging goal, *a creatively empowering leader*, and a collaborative, biblically
honoring community."

Another Fatal Team Error

One mistake that will cause a team to wither or simply fall apart is if it
has a leader who is primarily focused on holding on to power. Teams don't
need empowered leaders but leaders who are truly empowering. Great team
leaders know that their opportunity to serve a church and ministry team is
a great privilege. They want to make their mark not by controlling the team
but by challenging, facilitating, and empowering the people on the team to
realize their full potential for God's kingdom purposes.

To review and move ahead a step further, here are the first three teaming errors:

> Fatal Teaming Error #1: When a team is undervalued.
> Fatal Teaming Error #2: When a team is underchallenged.
> Fatal Teaming Error #3: A leader who holds onto power.

One of the most important questions for a teaming leader to ask is
this: Is my leadership more about my own power or empowering the team?
What could I do to better serve my team and team members? How could I
challenge our team more effectively?

> A team leader holds on to power when she monopolizes the team
> discussions.

> A team leader holds on to power when he fails to delegate respon-
> sibilities to the team regularly.

> A team leader holds on to power when he has to oversee every
> church project.

> A team leader holds on to power when she doesn't include the
> team or staff on the interview process for new hires.

The Challenge of Teambuilding

Teambuilding is challenging work. After all, to propose to develop
groups of people who are effectively working together in a collaborative environment requires diligence and vigilance. Stephen Macchia has led teams
for years throughout New England and has said that:

Teams are very difficult to create. They are tougher to motivate. They are impossible to predict. They can be challenging to lead. They can inspire greatness and they can embody pettiness. They can gel quickly and they can splinter apart overnight. They are filled with people who are unique in their backgrounds, hurts, needs, joys, desires, gifts, aspirations, and call. To get a diverse group of people working on the same page is the ongoing priority and challenge for leaders.[2]

Teams are not a fad. They are here and now and, I believe, here to stay. They are without a doubt the preferred work environment of emerging generations. Leonard Sweet has said that:

The future belongs not so much to movers and shakers but to leaders who can work in teams. In fact, the movers and shakers of postmodern culture are teams, which must become the dominant model for ministry and mission. There are no more clergy and laity. There are only ministers. [An essential skill for navigating today's culture as a church leader] is the art of making every member as good a minister as you are endeavoring to be.[3]

But just what are the key teambuilding skills? What are the key characteristics of the true teaming leader?

The Characteristics of a Teaming Leader: Essential Qualities

The teaming church requires not just leadership, but a certain kind of leader. While hierarchical leaders are one-dimensional and power driven, teaming leaders are multidimensional and empowering.

Teaming leadership is not just a skill you learn, it is an art you develop. While understanding certain principles about teams and teambuilding is important, teaming leadership is learned on the field of life and ministry. It involves understanding people and how they best work together. Here are some of the more vital characteristics of a person who is best prepared to lead a team:

The teaming leader draws circles of collaboration grounded by the goal of authentic biblical unity.

Teaming leadership involves much more than just getting a job done in the church; it is about creating a culture in which communion, community, and collaborations can occur within a context of worship.

So much of our lives is spent asking God to answer our prayers, wouldn't it be nice for a change to consider some of the ones Jesus prayed and to see if we can help answer his prayers? One prayer he prayed, referred to by theologians as the "High Priestly Prayer of Christ," was spoken during the final week of his earthly ministry. Among them was the prayer: "I have given them the glory that you gave me, *that they may be one as we are one*—I in them and you in me—so that they may be brought to complete unity. Then the world will know that you sent me and have loved them even as you have loved me" (John 17:22-23 NIV, italics mine).

Teaming leaders are not just people with a project or two to complete; they are agents of biblical unity. They are the people who cultivate communities in which the presence of God can be experienced, the glory of God seen, and the gospel of Jesus Christ portrayed. That's not just organizational—it's powerful!

The teaming leader recognizes that a team is much more than a mere group; it is an honoring circle that reflects the nature of the Trinity.

Over the past one hundred years, in a reaction to evolutionary theory, many Christians have relegated ideas of the *Imago Dei* (or "the image of God") to an individualistic view. For years many have thought that the image of God is something we see when we look in a mirror. However, it is vital that we recognize that a key part of understanding our being made in the image of God is how we experience that image within the context of community and collaborations.

Teaming leaders shift their environment from hierarchical values to interdependent ones. They draw circles of unity, not triangles of hierarchy. They don't move people ahead by pushing them around, they do so by drawing them in.

> Teamwork is essential for a productive organization. Collaboration is needed to develop the commitment and skills of employees, solve problems, and respond to environmental pressures. Fostering collaboration is not just a nice idea. It is the key that leaders use to unlock the energies and talents available in their organizations.[4]

The Trinity is the ultimate example of community. Creation itself was a collaborative effort among the members of the Trinity ("let *us* make man in *our* image"—Gen 1:26 NIV, italics mine). Teaming leaders take their cues in building community from the actions and responses of the members of the Trinity to one another throughout scripture.

Jesus requested that his followers would come into a relational oneness; not only a unity, but also *a certain kind* of unity—"one, even as you and I are one." Christ sought to nurture a team or community for each of his followers that was characteristic of the place in which he thrived (that is, the Trinitarian fellowship).

Whatever significance you see in your community, whatever importance you attribute to your team, it is probably worth so much more than you yet see.

The teaming leader consistently studies, communicates, and affirms how everything and everyone in the circle connects.

Perhaps the main picture of a disconnected church in the New Testament was the Corinthian church. After all, if the big idea of his first letter to the church at Corinth could be whittled down to a declarative statement from the apostle Paul, it would probably read, and I'll paraphrase: "Don't compare yourselves; don't condemn others; don't condone sin; don't compete with each other; and don't campaign for your own interests. Rather, commune with God and one another!"

As a teaming leader, Paul paints a vivid picture of how the roles of believers and team members differ but how they have in common the idea of being a part of a greater body. Paul carries the metaphor further in specificity as he enjoins the concept of the "supporting ligament" in Ephesians:

> Instead, by speaking the truth with love, let's grow in every way into Christ, who is the head. The whole body grows from him, as it is joined and held together by all the *supporting ligaments*. The body makes itself grow in that it builds itself up with love as each one does their part. (Eph 4:15-16 CEB, italics mine)

While body parts such as the heart and the head get much more press and attention in sermons and seminars, Paul draws out a less-familiar reference—the "supporting ligaments." Physiologically, ligaments are the tough fibrous tissues that connect our bones together and create joints. In a real sense, it is our ligaments that hold our frame together. Paul draws upon this image to urge the Ephesian believers to work hard at being "joined," "held together," and built "up." What Paul is appealing to is that believers do a better job of not only working, but also working *together*, as a team.

In fact, the article in the *Harvard Business Review* cited in chapter 3 describes the type of person who makes the "best type of team member."[5] Interestingly, they are described as "charismatic connectors" or as people who don't get isolated in the organization but circle around engaging their coworkers frequently in sincere but brief dialog. They don't play favorites, but endeavor to communicate equally and are committed to giving everyone a chance to add to the conversation. While they ask engaging questions, they also take ample time to listen intently. In an intensive study conducted at MIT, the researchers "found that the more of these charismatic connectors a team had, the more successful it was."[6]

The teaming leader understands and respects the paradoxes and dynamic tensions of the effective team circle.

Teaming leadership is not something owned, possessed, or grasped; it is held with respect and shared. The person who really gets it in this area of teaming leadership, who really understands a biblical view of servant leadership, realizes that the higher up you go as a leader, the more you have to surrender, give away, or lose.

In more triangular hierarchical models, leaders tend to ask themselves questions such as: Who's on first? Who is the lead dog? Who's in charge here? Who goes first? Who will sit at the head table? Who gets to swing the gavel?

In more circular teaming models, leaders tend to ask a different set of questions, such as: Who most needs my help? What can I do to help my team members succeed? How can I serve my team and team members? What would be one way I could make my team members feel appreciated and honored? What would make us tighter and more effective as a team?

While hierarchical leadership is a simple way to lead, teaming leadership requires vigilance, thought, and constant communication. Paul's call to the Ephesians to "maintain the unity of the Spirit in the bond of peace" (4:3) is no cakewalk. Sometimes, on the contrary, it is bull work!

While hierarchical leadership may be more clear-cut and immediately definitive, it is predicated upon the whims, notions, instincts, mood swings, and wishes of just one person, one mind, one point of view, and one will. That's all. That is incredibly limiting to an organization and to a church. Teaming leadership is more nuanced. It requires the balancing of dynamic tensions and paradoxes. Here are just a few:

Paradoxes—Teaming Leadership Involves:

- Leading, by serving
- Organizing, by delegating
- Building trust, by showing it
- Exercising authority, by giving it away
- Not giving right orders, but asking right questions
- Owning up to your own mistakes and sharing your successes with the team

The teaming leader is the lead goaltender in the circle.

Teaming leaders help teams define, refine, remember, and measure their goals, and to celebrate each one achieved. In professional football, coaches focus on a few things over and over again. Among them: training the team players in the necessary skills of the game, helping the team members become team players, observing team performance (that is, watching one game film after another), and keeping an eye on the statistics (that is, the record of progress toward goals—both team and individual progress).

On a ministry team, wise team leaders give attention to goaltending. They keep an eye on the goals and the progress (or lack of progress) toward them. When the goals are being met or exceeded, offering affirmations and support to help keep on the game plan or strategy is the teaming leader's focus. When the goals are not being met and the team is failing or falling behind, the teaming leader wants to find this out at the earliest moment possible so that the team can revisit the goals, strategies, and systems and find ways to make necessary midcourse corrections. And, lastly:

Teaming leaders don't boss from the top down. They come alongside the team within the circle and lead by their facilitating and coaching influence.

Almost everything about leadership tempts you to go it alone, to move to hierarchical and autocratic forms by default. Every time a conflict emerges, for instance, some leaders are tempted to just deal with it swiftly by pushing their weight around or exercising their privileges as a leader. The temptation to turn *boss* on your team will come and sometimes be hard to resist.

This is not to say that leaders or teaming leaders should *never* wield their authority. Sometimes it is necessary, for example, due to a team member who steps outside of the good faith values of the team. Once that person stops playing by the rules and road map of the team, it may require stronger measures to bring the member back to her senses. But, if you have to step into that arena from time to time, be determined not to stay there. If you stay there too long, you may find it virtually impossible to return to a community of trust and collegiality. Remember, tyranny can quickly usurp *koinonia*.

Redefining Leadership

A teaming leader gets to redefine the term "leadership" within his or her community.

Teams cannot stand to be run by bosses; rather, they must be led by facilitating leaders or coaching leaders. There is a huge difference between a boss and a leader. Consider these contrasts:

Bosses vs. Leaders

A boss creates fear.	A leader creates trust.
A boss says "I."	A leader says "We."
*Boss*ism creates resentment.	*Leader*ship breeds enthusiasm.
A boss knows how.	A leader shows how.
A boss fixes blame.	A leader fixes mistakes.
A boss pushes people.	A leader draws people.
*Boss*ism makes work a drudgery.	*Leader*ship makes work interesting.
A boss relies on authority.	A leader relies on cooperation.
A boss drives.	A leader leads.

Moses, the Teaming Consultant

Moses faced another challenge toward moving a nation into the Promised Land. This time, however, he put together a team of researchers or spies who were sent to explore the land of Canaan.

The numbers of people under Moses' care had vastly multiplied, "the burden of the people" (Num 11:17) had increased even more, and Moses acknowledged, "How can I alone bear the load and burden of you and your strife?" (Deut 1:12 NASB).

Fortunately, Moses no longer needed a career counselor, leadership consultant, or more advice from his father-in-law. He had learned and grown as a leader and saw it as a time for teams. He was learning about his limitations and his options for leading people. "Now, for each of your tribes, choose wise, discerning, and well-regarded individuals," Moses said. "I will appoint them as your leaders" (Deut 1:13 CEB). This team of leaders not only shared the various duties of transporting the people of God to the Promised Land, they also did so in a just and fair manner.

Not only had Moses grown as a teaming leader; his confidence had increased along the way. You can hear it in his words:

> Then you responded, "Your plan is a good one." So I took the wise and respected men you had selected from your tribes and appointed them to serve as judges and officials over you. Some were responsible for a thousand people, some for a hundred, some for fifty, and some for ten. At that time I instructed the judges, "You must hear the cases of your fellow Israelites and the foreigners living among you. Be perfectly fair in your decisions and impartial in your judgments. Hear the cases of those who are poor as well as those who are rich. Don't be afraid of anyone's anger, for the decision you make is God's decision. Bring me any cases that are too difficult for you, and I will handle them." At that time I gave you instructions about everything you were to do. (Deut 1:14-18 NLT)

Empowering Leadership

True teaming leaders do not obsess over their own power and control. Instead, they find great satisfaction in using their entrusted powers to empower others, their team members, and their staff. Leonard Sweet has written that:

> Leadership is less about employing people than empowering people. Leadership is less about controlling people than releasing them. This does not mean that other people will not put their lives in your hands. But the whole purpose of an air-traffic "controller" is not to keep planes on the land, but to get them off the ground and into the sky. What do "controllers" do? They clear pilots for takeoff.[7]

103

The control towers manned by teaming leaders are not thrones, but bleachers on a playing field. You can tell who the teaming leaders are. They are the ones on the edges of their seats cheering the team on the loudest!

A Teaming Leader Interview, Large Church: Jeff Sellers

Jeff Sellers, campus pastor, Victory Church@Lakeside Village-Cobb Theatre, Lakeland, Florida.

Jeff Sellers is the campus pastor of Victory Church@Lakeside Village— a branch campus of Victory Church, a megachurch in central Florida. The senior pastor is Wayne Blackburn. This thriving congregation meets in a local movie theater.

Q: What do you look for in a new staff member?

A: First of all, I look for someone who is compatible with the DNA of the local church. Second, I want to like them. Actually during their interview weekend, I have them stay in my home, so I can get to know them better.

Q: How can you tell when a group has turned into a true team?

A: When you don't have to push them. When they show up for the big game and are ready to play. When they are doing life together. Teams function best when the players know one another.

Q: What undermines teams?

A: When people put who they are or what they are doing ahead of the church. At that point it is no longer about everybody wins—but I'm going to win. You want to find strong leaders for your team, but it is challenging to find those tempered enough to work with a team.

Q: What was one of the best teams you were ever a part of?

A: It was the pastoral team I served with in Palatka, Florida, at a church of about 400 to 450.

Q: What made it such a great team?

A: The team was young (we were all in our late twenties), talented, and confident. Everybody would take a bullet for the others. We intentionally socialized together. We babysat for each other. We ate loads of pizza after evening church services. We all knew we were young and probably didn't know much, but man we were hopeful! The church could feel the love we had for each other. Our team was contagious.

Q: What are the characteristics of a great team leader?

A: The ability to call out greatness on the team is one. Also, you never want the team to wonder if you are second guessing them. It is important to speak up for them in public and to only confront them in private. They must know that you as a leader have their back and are going to support and equip them. Don't ever send them out onto the field without the right equipment. Set them up to be successful.

Drawing Your Circle

Questions to Ask Your Team

1. What does it take to be a true teaming leader?

2. In what ways was Moses both a bad and good example of a true teaming leader?

3. How important is unity to a great team? What role does it play in the process? What does it take to maintain it?

4. Take another look at the list of paradoxes in this chapter. Which ones do you feel the most on your team? Explain.

5. What will effective goaltending require on your team?

6. Can a boss lead a team? Explain.

Chapter Seven

Essential Skills of Teaming Leaders: Unleashing Team Brilliance

*Find out how God has designed each team
member and keep them in their strengths.*
—*Terry Storch, Digerati Leader, Pastor, LifeChurch.tv/YouVersion.com*

Outdo one another in showing honor.
—*Romans 12:10 (ESV)*

One of the best ways to strengthen your team is to sharpen your teaming skills. The effectiveness your team exhibits has a direct relationship to the way you lead it. Effective team leadership requires much more than resolve; it involves reflection and intentional efforts to broaden and grow your teaming skills and those of your team members.

Research and experience has convinced me that great teams engage in a few essential best practices that inform and shape their collaborations. Study and engage these values and habits and your team will thrive. Overlook or ignore them and your team will do what so many end up doing— grow tired, sluggish, and ineffective.

Sharpen your skills and you will strengthen your team.

Church specialist Leonard Sweet notes that today:

> In [effective] ecclesiastical ecosystems, people at the lowest levels must
> be given every decision-making power and entrepreneurial boost to

rise to the top; creativity in all staff, including those at the lowest level, must be given free reign; teams must be encouraged to be self-organizing; power and authority must be shared by everyone.[1]

Whereas yesterday's leader often only thought in terms of projects and goals (What is the next project? How is it coming? What will it take to make it succeed?), today's leader is not only focused on projects and goals but also on culture (What kind of leadership environment are we creating? What values do we embrace and convey?). Their thoughts are not primarily attuned to the microfocus of the next program, but to the macroenvironment of the community, values, and culture that will nurture the people who carry out the projects.

Instead of merely asking, "Will people like this upcoming event?" the teaming leader asks, "Is this a culture in which people can thrive?"

Instead of asking, "What will it take to grow this church bigger?" the teaming leader asks, "What will it take to grow these souls larger?" Because they know that it will take larger souls to grow a church.

Instead of asking, "How can I show the congregation my leadership strengths?" the teaming leader asks, "How can I help each member realize his or her God-given strengths?"

Instead of asking, "How can I draw a bigger crowd?" the teaming leader asks, "How can I draw stronger circles of faith, community, and service to others?"

The values of the teaming leader inspire a set of practices that serve to create a culture in which teams are the lively networks in which people thrive. The work of the teaming leader is helping ensure that the teams and the team members feel valued, focused, and interactive; and that they collaborate and evaluate effectively.

In a hierarchical structure, the organization is seldom better than the leader. His strengths become its strengths; his weaknesses, its weaknesses. However, in a true team model, as long as the team leader fulfills her key functions, the team can employ the team leader's strengths and even rise far beyond them. Also, a functioning team can quite ably compensate for his areas of weakness. Katzenbach and Smith say:

> The team leader is seldom the primary determinant of team performance. Clearly, team leaders have an important role, especially at the beginning. . . . A wide variety of people and personalities can lead. . . . However, effective team leaders are characterized mostly by attitude and belief, as in, "I believe in our purpose, and I know we cannot achieve it with individual contributions and accountability alone. We must succeed or fail together as a team."[2]

Practices of True Teaming

What, then, are the primary practices of true teaming leaders and team members? In other words, what habits constitute the practices of those committed to cultivating a true teaming culture?

Teaming Creates a Culture of Convincing Honor

The teaming leader considers himself the CHO, the chief honoring officer. Teaming leaders see their role as the people most responsible to initiate and cultivate an environment of sincere and strong affirmation. They have come to know that encouragement and building up others is what helps make a church culture vibrant and buoyant, even irresistible. They know that it is honor that helps the team feel valued. And, remember, honor is much different than flattery. The last thing team members need to succeed in their roles and ministry relationships is flattery. While flattery is the insincere practice of telling people what we think they want to hear, honoring is the quite sincere discipline of seeing people as they truly are in the eyes of God and telling them what they need to hear. While flattery puffs up, honor (or love) builds up (1 Cor 8:1). Flattery is political; honor is powerful. Flattery focuses on what people can do; honor focuses on what God is doing through people. Flattery strokes the ego; honor strengthens the soul.

A team leader showing honor to the team members is actually essential to communication itself. Amy Edmondson, professor at Harvard University, says, "Research does show . . . that leaders can promote speaking up [among team members] through particular behaviors and actions. Most important, when leaders explicitly communicate that they respect (that is, honor) employees, it makes it easier for employees to volunteer their knowledge."[3]

Teaming Emphasizes Compelling Goal Setting

Teaming leaders are consistently aware of the need the team has for a carrot, or the focal point of a desired end that unites the team's efforts and stretches its abilities to the point of trusting God. The teaming leader keeps the goal in their sights, on their mind, and before the team. They are constantly asking questions about the goal, such as:

- Is our goal big enough? Is it man-sized or God-sized?
- Is our goal clear enough?
- How will we know when we have accomplished our goal?
- How much of the goal has already been accomplished? 5 percent? 50 percent? 75 percent? How much?
- How will our goal serve the purposes of God's kingdom?

Teaming leaders know that compelling goals help the team focus. The individual gifts, strengths, temperaments, and interests of a team can pull their thoughts and focus in a hundred different directions. Only shared faith and shared goals help them to serve God side-by-side with a common vision. The wise leader keeps the carrot out in front of the team. As she does, she will find that drawing the team toward a desired goal is much more effective than pushing them toward their job description or list of objectives. Yesterday's churches were focused on job descriptions; today's growing churches are focused on great teams with great goals working in a great environment of great trust.

Bobby Gruenewald, the founder of YouVersion.com, says, "As a leader, I try to get altitude in my perspective and help them catch it." His associate and the team leader of their Digerati team, Terry Storch, says, "We have lots of talks about our capacity as a team."

Teaming Prioritizes Clear Communication

One of the universal truths of communication and information (and vision, for that matter) is that it tends to leak. In other words, no sooner do we receive information than do we already begin to lose (or confuse) some of it as well, which is a bit ironic in an age of information. Wise leaders focus on more than periodic announcements; they create systems of communication that are rapid, repetitive, and strategically diverse. Instead of simply putting information in a newsletter that everyone is expected to read, teaming leaders carry out multilayered communications that do not just float down from hierarchies, but that rapidly fire among the various systems of the church. Clear communication helps the team understand what they need to know.

Teaming Nurtures Consistent Trust

A team's sense of trust is directly related to their sense of trust of their team leader. Trust is a powerful and delicate component of any church's (or other organization's) life. It is as integral to a church or organization as it is to a marriage or friendship. When trust is built over time, the strength of the team becomes palpable. When trust is violated or undervalued, the frustrations and weakness of the team become equally forceful.

Trust is what helps the team collaborate with one another. It is the sense of mutual trust that helps reduce the individualization of the team and move it toward more communitarian and collaborative practices.

Teaming Maintains Corporate Accountability

When some people think of team accountability, they picture a player who is accountable to a coach. But, true team or corporate accountability is something more. It involves each individual on the team feeling not only accountable to the team leader, pastor or coach, but even more so to the team itself.

It is one thing to hold a person accountable to one leader. That is a simple approach, but it is also time intensive. Hierarchical leadership can often be overcontrolling and can become unhealthy, leading to overly dependent workers or employees. Shared or corporate accountability is an approach that requires more skill and intentionality.

Teaming leaders work hard at nurturing a sense of corporate accountability because they know that it helps the team evaluate its current state and progress.

In Search of Team Brilliance

You may have heard the old saying that none of us is nearly as smart (or as wise) as all of us. Proverbs 15:22 says, "Plans fail for lack of counsel, but with many advisers they succeed" (NIV). The teaming leader knows that it is simply not enough to have a set of individually designed plans with which to proceed. It is important that the plans emerge amidst an environment that is communication rich, counsel filled, and collaboration saturated. In fact, wise team leaders regularly solicit the suggestions, opinions, and concerns of their team members. They know that God-sized goals and plans will require more insight and wisdom than one mind can muster alone; it will need the Spirit-inspired contemplations and interactions of a set of sanctified minds.

Teaming leaders are the caretakers of the team brain trust and seek to provoke and inspire these collective minds to apply themselves to their best thinking. Teaming tasks will require teaming leaders to ask teaming questions in order to achieve teaming results.

Tapping team brilliance will require some effort and collaborative skill development on the part of leaders, with sometimes excruciating effort. Each of us can hit sticking points of creativity, new ideas, new ways of solving problems, or approaches to people development. Teaming leaders have to help teams push through those stuck seasons and move, and sometimes drill, further in their interactions, discussions, and ministry beta tests to the places of discovering and uncovering insights and strategies laced with teaming brilliance.

"The purposes of a person's heart are deep waters, / but one who has insight draws them out" (Prov 20:5 NIV).

Collaborative Skills—Bringing Out Team Brilliance

What kinds of spurs or skills does your team need in order to unleash its areas of brilliance? Here are seven practices that teaming leaders regularly use to bring out the brilliance in their teams. Each one is an important skill that the most effective teaming leaders learn to use and continually sharpen.

Teaming Skill #1: Asking

Of all the skills of the teaming leader, perhaps the one that is most lacking today is the ability to ask effective questions. While a good question can open a conversation, a great question can open a team's soul. In other words, questions about sports, hobbies, the weather, and so on can get things rolling in a conversation. More pointed and provocative questions can unearth poignant and freeing truths, as well as powerful ideas, insights, and innovations.

In fact, effective questions are so important that I have written a number of books on the subject.[4] It is vital that leaders master the skill of asking, the teaming leader must learn how to turn a good question into a great one. This involves understanding what makes a great question truly great. The right question asked of the right person at the right time can do much to draw out insight and creativity. The wise leader of teams today uses questions to challenge and inspire his team to greatness.

Asking, rather than telling, has become a key to leadership excellence and success. Leadership expert Peter Drucker noted that the leader of the past may have been a person who knew how to tell, but the leader of the future will be a person who knows how to ask. With the growing complexity and speed of change in the world, the traditional hierarchical model of leadership that worked yesterday will not work tomorrow. The leader simply won't know enough to adequately tell people what to do. No one person can master all the data needed to address the complex issues that confront today's organizations.

Church (and business) leaders are so accustomed to telling and teaching (and preaching) that we may need to be retrained to ask. Chris Argyris says:

> [We must] balance our natural tendency toward advocacy (explaining, communicating, teaching) with a less spontaneous behavior: inquiry (expressions of curiosity followed by genuine listening). A useful discipline for leaders is to force moments of reflection, asking themselves and then others, "Is this the only way to see the situation? What might I be missing?" Such exploration . . . is critical to successful teaming.[5]

Michael Dell, founder and leader of the computer company that bears his name, is a strong believer in the power of questions. "Asking a lot of questions opens new doors to new ideas, which ultimately contributes to your competitive edge," he says. Dell is also a big believer in learning from everyone in the company.[6]

Michael Marquardt says when we ask the right questions of our team members it can lead to beneficial results, such as:

- **causing** the person to focus and to stretch; creating deeper reflection;

- **challenging** taken-for-granted assumptions that prevent people from acting in new and forceful ways;

- **leading** people to breakthrough thinking;

- **finding** the keys that open the door to great solutions;

- **enabling** people to better view their situation;

- **opening** doors in the mind and getting people to think more deeply;

- **testing** assumptions and causing individuals to explore why they act in the way that they do as well as why they choose to take action; and

- **generating** positive and powerful action.[7]

112

Teaming Skill #2: Listening

It just may be that the best way to make a person feel truly honored is to listen to them with rapt and sincere attentiveness. The most important interest rate in our day and age may be the ability you and I have as leaders to truly "not [look] to your own interests but each of you to the interests of the others" (Phil 2:4 NIV). You can't do that without asking some questions and doing some listening. Few practices are more meaningful than the person who will give you undivided attention; few oversights are more demeaning than when someone makes you feel that listening is an unwanted chore.

One reason some groups never turn into true teams is that they are never truly heard by the team leader. It is one thing to ask your team members questions; it is altogether another thing to truly listen to them. Really hearing your team involves deep listening or what some refer to as "reflective listening." That means what some have called listening with the third ear. This kind of deep listening involves:

- **Eye contact.** No staring down a person, but setting your focus on their words and nonverbal cues as you listen; paying close attention, which is deeply affirming.

- **Verbal following.** Using short and sincere words and phrases to assure the listener that you are not only tracking verbally but viscerally, as well. ("Yes" . . . "I see" . . . "mmm, hmm" . . . "alright" . . . "I follow you" . . . and so forth.)

- **Rapt posture.** While you may not necessarily be on the edge of your seat over every word, make sure that you are poised for active listening and responding. Sitting up straight and even leaning slightly forward conveys attentiveness.

- **Follow-up questions.** Some statements of your team members are intentionally laced with the hope that you will probe more fully into their thoughts, suggestions, and opinions. Using follow-up questions will help you to do so.

Teaming Skill #3: Reflecting

If there is one skill overlooked in our day and age it is thinking. By that, I mean taking the time to think and to reflect on our lives, our relationships, our families, our work, our ideas, our challenges, our opportunities, our strengths, and our weaknesses. Socrates said, "The unexamined life is not worth living." In the same manner, "The unexamined team is not worth leading or following."

Thinking is the period of time and interaction on a team that comes in between our research and our plans of action. Thinking is the rumination that carries us from speculation to determination. Team thinking is the filter that purifies individual spurts of inspiration and turns them into forceful rivers of purposeful and timely teaming goals and strategies.

If teams are determined to catch fire and accomplish things of greatness, it will involve a process that includes reflection. In a sense, the ideas and opinions that teams and team members uncover are the wood that is placed in the fireplace. Reflection is the process of striking several matches and fanning the flame until the wood catches fire. The full flame is the idea or vision being owned and lived out by the team. Without reflection all you have is a pile of wood. Reflection as a team tests the kind of wood to see exactly what will catch fire.

Teaming Skill #4: Disagreeing

One of the worst experiences a team can have is to always agree. How boring is that? If a team is always in constant agreement, it is because of one of four reasons:

- Group members are intimidated by their leader and afraid to express their opinions.
- People are not being honest about their true opinions and ideas.
- The mix of temperaments on the team is unbalanced.
- Apathy exists on the team.

Jim Kling says, "Conflict is inevitable, and it can be the single best fuel for the creative fire" on a team. "Without it, teams become stagnant and good ideas wither and die."[8] Conflict is a welcomed teacher on a mature team. Experienced team members and leaders know that conflicts are overlooked at the detriment of the organization and the team. Conflicts faced honestly and openly more often than not serve as a directive for the team to improve some aspect of the team's function or of the church or organization they represent.

When team members passionately and honestly weigh in, suddenly the meeting gets interesting. Great teams will face times of great disagreement.

It is a part of the price you pay to be a part of an open and honest work environment. In order to discover and uncover the best ideas, periods of disagreement and team conflict will happen. They are par for the course. Don't be alarmed when you experience them and help your team not to be alarmed, but be aware. No elephant breeding, please!

Wise teaming leaders see conflicts when they emerge on a team and call them for what they are. As long as conflict is identified, it does not have to be feared. In a sense, when we experience pain in our bodies, we are acknowledging a conflict: something is out of harmony; something doesn't work as it should. As a result, it gets our attention and if we cannot fix or help it—we find someone who can.

Noted team and management specialist, Peter Senge, says, "In great teams conflict becomes productive. The free flow of conflicting ideas is critical for creative thinking, for discovering new solutions no one individual would have come up with on his own."[9]

James taught us to "count it all joy" when we fall into times of trial and conflict (James 1:2). His advice helps the believer zoom out a bit when a conflict occurs, and realize that a sovereign God is using it to work a greater glory (2 Cor 4:17). In other words, conflicts alert us to areas within our bodies (and within the body of Christ) that need our attention. There is no need to fear them; yet, there is every reason to study them and consider the wisest course of action and response.

In his book, *Wild At Heart*, John Eldridge urges readers to "let people feel the weight of your person." What did he mean by that? Well, I believe he was saying that in order to give your best to a relationship, to a church, or to a church team, you have to let your ideas, thoughts, and opinions be known, no matter how conflicting they may be.

The wise teaming leader won't just ask, "What do you think?" but "What do you really think?"

The wise teaming leader won't just ask, "How could we improve next time?" but "Where did we blow it this time?"

The wise (and seasoned) teaming leader won't just ask, "What is a strength of my leadership on this team that you appreciate?" Instead she asks, "What is something I can do to better serve or facilitate this team?"

Teaming Skill #5: Storytelling

Our workplaces, schools, and homes are full of stories. People long to be a part of something larger, of God's bigger story. But how can they enter that story unless someone tells them? Churches and church teams have stories going on within the lives of people all around them that are just begging to be told.

Here are four significant aspects of stories to recognize.

- *Your story is who you are.* God not only created you; he allowed the specific circumstances that have shaped your story to come about. You are the story he has written. It is God's grace that shapes you into a "new creation" in Christ (2 Cor 5:17). You are a person with a story to tell. Your team has stories to tell. Tell them.

- *Your story is not meant to be private, but public.* Telling your story matters to God and to those who need to hear.

- *Your story is not about your goodness, but God's goodness to you, your church, and your team.* Remember, the peaks and valleys of a story only add to the plot and tension. They can be compelling. Some details may be best left untold, but Jesus has paid too high a price for us to hide the honest telling of our story.

- Telling your stories overcomes Satan. Ultimately, it is Satan who wants to keep Christians quiet. He wants to downplay and minimize your God-given story. Revelation, however, reveals that the way we overcome Satan is "by the blood of the Lamb and by the word of [our] testimony [that is, our God story]" (Rev 12:11 ESV). Your stories and your team's stories are powerful tools for community building and goal achieving.

Teaming Skill #6: Deciding

If teaming leaders are not careful, the process of asking, listening, and thinking can lead to dead-end deliberations. As important as it is to ask thoroughly, listen thoroughly, and reflect thoroughly, it is equally important to decide in a timely and definitive manner. While groups may simply choose to discuss and debate, it takes a team to decide. While reflection opens up an array of possibilities to a team, deciding turns those possibilities into a plan of action. And while a team should not hurry to a decision too soon, it also dare not wait too long. Smart teams strike while the iron and the idea are hot!

Here are some questions that can help a leader turn the best ideas into action:

- Are we ready to make a decision?
- What would it take to turn this idea into a reality?
- Who is the best person to lead the charge on this action step?
- How soon can this be up and running?

Team Skill #7: Praying Together

Of all the practices a team can use, the one that will define them the most as a true ministry team is praying together. As Christians, we know that prayer is vital to our faith experience and our dependency upon God. But prayer is also the language of the soul. When we pray together—really pray—our deepest needs, hopes, concerns, and burdens have a way of emerging. Listening to one another's voices and souls engages the presence of God as a way of not only bringing good ideas but also God ideas!

More Than Skills

Teaming skills are the tools that help a leader shape and turn a group of people into a team. Just as Moses once learned, teaming leadership consists of engaging a new approach and a new set of skills. These skills enable teaming leaders to truly tap the brilliance within their teams. In order to keep a teaming church moving ahead and growing, however, it requires something more than just a new set of skills; it involves a new mind-set, a teaming mind-set—one that is vividly rooted in the insights and images of teams in the Bible. The pictures are vivid and vital to developing your ministry team.

Drawing Your Circle

Questions to Ask Your Team

1. What are some of the strengths (or areas of brilliance) that your team possesses?

2. What questions does you team need to be asked frequently to help keep it on its toes?

3. Complete this sentence: "When I am talking to our team, I really want people to _____."

4. When was the last time your team really disagreed or worked through some conflict? Did you do so well? Explain. Did the conflict push the team apart or pull it together?

5. How good is your team at discussing and airing their various thoughts, viewpoints, and ideas?

6. How good is your team at making timely decisions?

Once Upon
a Team—
Scene Four

Overtime

"We're in luck! She just started reading a good book," Glenn said.

"Your wife?" Scott responded.

"Yes, my wife. She said 'just take your time.'"

"Are you sure? Glenn, I don't want to keep you from any commitments."

"No, Scott. Really, this is fine. I told her that a new friend of mine needs another hour and she said 'just take your time.' So, you know what that means?"

"No. What?" Scott said, glad to be referred to as Glenn's "friend."

"That means it must be a *really* good book!" Glenn laughed.

"Sounds like it. Maybe I need to encourage my wife to read more! When you find out the title of it—let me know. She could use something to help her get her mind off all of these church issues."

"So, where were we? Your church just feels 'stuck'; is that right?"

"That's exactly right. No one really wants to admit it. In fact, a big part of me doesn't want to say it, and especially to someone who works at the church right down the street from me; but, nonetheless, that makes it no less true."

"Scott, I appreciate your candor."

"Honest to a fault, huh?"

"I don't know about that," Glenn said, "but I find your focus on truth to be refreshing. But, are you as honest as that when you meet with your teams at church? And, with your board?"

"No way; I'm not that honest with them. Why? Should I be?"

"Of course," Glenn said. "What is the alternative?"

"Well, the pastor I trained under years ago told me that no matter what problems you face in the church you lead, never let on that you are concerned or at all worried about what you see. He said that a pastor must maintain what he called an 'even straight.' I guess he meant don't ever let people see you sweat."

"I tried that approach myself for a season as a young pastor, and do you know what?"

"What's that?"

"It didn't work. Not for me, at least. The more I worked at putting up a good front, the more I felt myself kind of falling apart on the inside and the more I saw my staff drifting apart on the outside."

"But," Scott continued, "I've heard it said that you have to guard your staff from the hard truths and realities. You know, focus on the positive; just keep pumping the good news their way and deal with the bad news on your own."

"Sounds like a setup for a breakdown, if you ask me."

"Really?"

"Yes. Really! Listen, Scott, you are the one who called and asked for me to meet with you, right?"

"Sure did."

"Well, at the risk of this being our last meeting—and I certainly hope it won't be—I am going to tell you something I wish my leaders and pastors had told me many years sooner."

"What's that?"

"Tell your teams the truth. Candor and honesty are friends of true teams and teaming leaders. In fact, teams can never focus nor partner effectively until they see their goals and obstacles, their strengths and weaknesses clearly."

"That sounds right. I have just never really seen the church operate that way."

"I didn't either, until about twenty years ago. And, interestingly enough, that is when I really started enjoying pastoring, and that's the time the church started to grow in many ways."

"What brought the change?"

Glenn looked around the café and smiled. "Actually, it was in a setting much like this one and in a meeting I had."

"With another pastor or mentor?"

"Actually, it was with an older man, a layman, in the church. An old bridge builder named Ed."

"Bridge builder?"

"That's right; a bridge builder."

"You mean that metaphorically, right?"

"Oh, no. Ed for years was the foreman who oversaw the building of many bridges for the interstate highways in our region."

"So, a real bridge builder?"

"In more ways than he will ever know."

"What happened?"

"Well, Ed and I would periodically meet for breakfast just to connect as brothers in Christ. One thing I had noticed about Ed from the start was that he had a way of speaking his mind and not ever being too worried about what people thought."

"Oh, I know a few people like that in our church. I tread carefully around them," Scott said.

"Well, sometimes those truth tellers may turn out to be your best friends."

"So, did he have some truth to tell you that day?"

"Yes, he did. You see, a week or so before our scheduled meeting, I had gone through one of the most difficult weeks I had ever had as a pastor."

"What happened?"

"I had two staff members resign within one week of each other."

"Ouch!"

"I was working hard at quote-unquote maintaining an even straight and looking the part of the pastor who was on top of it. But, Ed asked me a question that morning: 'So, how are you doing this week, Pastor?' My response was quick and formulated: 'Oh, fine, Ed. Praise God! Just moving ahead and doing well.'"

"What did he say to that?"

"It wasn't just what he said; it was what he did. It's as if he could tell I wasn't being fully honest. He leaned over across the table, grabbed my forearm with his big calloused hand, looked me square in the eye and said, 'How are you really doing, Pastor? You're hurting, aren't you? I can see it. We all can see it.'"

"And you always hope they can't, right?" Scott said.

"Tell me about it. So, at that point, I said, 'What do you mean, Ed?' He responded, 'Pastor, we all know you have lost a couple of trusted staff members recently, and I can see that you are hurting. I just want you to know that I care and am praying for you, Pastor.'"

"Wow. Armor bearer time, huh?"

"Well," Glenn said, "Something happened I never expected. The more Ed talked, the more the tears just started streaming down my face. That's unusual for me. I'm not a big crier, but that brother in Christ saw the burden I was carrying and his concern gave me a place to unload some of it, although it was a bit uncomfortable for me. He tapped into something no one had dared approach."

"'Uncomfortable' is the right word. How did you work through that?"

"Ed looked me in the eyes and said, 'Pastor, if you try to carry all of that hurt and burden alone, you may try to get through it by yourself. But, if you will share with the church that you need our prayers and support as you seek God for wisdom during this challenging time, then we can come around you, pray for you, and support you. If you don't tell us, or at least some of us, we can't know how to help.' I learned something from Ed about teams and about churches that day."

"I'll bet. Kind of a whole paradigm shift, right?"

"Honestly, it was humbling and difficult to swallow."

Scott said, "You learned don't waste your energy or compromise your own soul pretending that everything is going well when you are a pastor facing some challenges. Is that it?"

"What I learned is that God not only uses great goals and dreams and visions to bring people together in families, in churches, and on teams, he also uses conflicts and challenges. When you pretend everything is peaceful and smooth when it isn't, then something disconcerting and disingenuous emerges. That something is called pretense and it destroys any sense of trust, community, or teamwork you may have. Candor is what fosters trust on a team and within a church, Scott. As teaming leaders, we don't have to sugarcoat or run from conflicts. We need to face them honestly and diligently."

"Wow. I never think of church conflicts as something positive. Did the things Ed said change the way you felt about your church problems?"

"They not only changed the way I felt about them, Ed's counsel to me that day changed the way I thought about and viewed conflicts. You see, Scott, before churches and teams become stuck in their function and experience, they tend to become stuck in their thinking and outlook. Conflict can actually become our friend, or something even better."

"That's okay—I have enough of those kinds of 'friends'!"

"Scott, have you ever heard the quote: 'Your friends will help you realize your potential, but your enemies will push you beyond it'?"

"No, I haven't."

"Conflicts are like that. They draw something out of us that otherwise we wouldn't have known was there. It's a determination like none other. It pushes us out of our stuckness," Glen said with a knowing grin.

It was quiet between Scott and Glenn for the first time since they had started talking. Glen knew some truths were starting to sink in. Scott was reflecting on the wisdom of his new friend and mentor.

Slowly, Scott asked, "So, how do I become unstuck as a leader?"

"Scott, I know you are feeling a big responsibility as a leader. But, let me tell you, it is good that you are facing some difficult truths, that you're not fooling yourself as a pastor. For starters, don't do too much of the thinking all on your own. The best thinking I have ever done as a pastor over the years has been on a team and within community. I call it team think."

"How do you do this team think thing?"

"I call it circle thinking."

"'Circle thinking'? What's that?"

"Really, it has to do with developing an adequate theology of relationships, community, and teams."

"Hold on, let me get my pen and journal. I can't take notes fast enough on my phone and I want to get all of this down. How is that again, a community theology or a team theology, right? What does that look like or sound like in a church the size of mine?" Scott asked.

"Well, your theology of teams or of community represents the biblical thinking you have done in this area. In a real sense your theology of teams develops the rootedness within your mind and heart that will empower you to build an authentic community and real biblical teams within your church over the long haul."

"I never really thought of the need to develop a theology of teams. When it comes to teams and leadership, honestly, I typically just go to the business section of the local bookstore and read what the latest CEOs are saying about it."

"That's fine, but while that will provide some technique and ideas for teaming, it won't develop the theological vision and motivation you need to build teams and a community that reflects the glory of God and is built on solid biblical principles."

"That sounds pretty profound," Scott said.

"It is. It may be that humanly speaking, few things are more profound. Scott, I believe that ministry teams and churches have the God-given potential of reflecting the very nature of God."

"How so?"

"Reflecting the Trinity; it's the Trinity," Glenn said. "The powerful and mysterious interrelation of the members of the Trinity is the picture of the ultimate team, the Divine Team. As we catch this and help our congregants catch it, something glorious begins to occur. We start to more truly reflect the image of God, the *Imago Dei.*"

"That is profound."

"It's worthy of some reflection. One thing I have discovered in my research is that some great theological minds such as Jonathan Edwards and Augustine placed a great emphasis on the importance of reflecting the Trinity with our human relationships and churches."

"I really want to study this and give it some more thought, but how does it play out practically, in my church and on my teams?"

"Well, for starters you have to embrace the conviction that we are smarter together as a team than we are as individuals. Proverbs 24:6 says: 'there is wisdom in a multitude of counselors.' Psalm 133 says, 'How good and pleasant it is when brothers dwell together in unity . . . For there does God command his blessing.'"

"That's one of my favorite verses."

"This verse challenges us to think. In order to act like a team, you have to start thinking as a team. It takes circle thinking, catching a great vision of how teams and communities of Christ can reflect the glory of God. How they reflect something of the Divine Team, the Circle of the Trinity."

"So you are really sold on this idea of a theology of teams and connecting it to the Trinity, aren't you?"

"Absolutely. I believe it is central to what church life and growth are all about."

"I guess I have never given much thought to the Trinity as a model for practical teaming ministry."

"Most pastors and leaders haven't."

"To me, the Trinity is such a mystery, so transcendent. I have never put much thought into seeing it as a ministry model."

"I am telling you, Scott, there is a world of practical insight for church ministry, team leadership, and the development of authentic community if we just take time to consider the roles and relationships of the Father, the Son, and the Holy Spirit."

"You've got me thinking; for sure."

A cell phone on the table rang out loud and Glenn saw that this time it wasn't his.

"Well, it looks like it is my wife calling this time," Scott said. "I will be just a minute."

"Take your time. I'm heading to the boy's room. All this coffee is catching up with me," Glenn smiled.

Part Three

Circle Thinking—
A Teaming Mind-Set

Mind maps have developed as a way people, and teams of people, think. In lieu of following a dated set of linear lists, teams and teaming leaders must learn to think outside of the box, but inside of the circle. The thing that connects a booster rocket to personal ingenuity is disciplined collaboration. While individuals may have great ideas, it takes a team to bring a great idea to life. While creativity is good and godly, left to itself it ends up like a starving artist. Connected to a network or community, the idea can be turned loose to thrive. In order to see teaming dynamics fully ignited within the life of a church, it will require more than a bunch of meetings; it will require a new kind of thinking—"circle thinking."

Chapter Eight

The
Divine Team

He who works for the honor of the one who sent him is a
man of truth; there is nothing false about him.
—*John 7:18 NIV*

Can you picture God holding a spotlight? If so, on whom is it shining? Following the spotlight reveals much about the way God wants us to live our lives, build up the body of Christ, and lead our teams.

One thing is for sure, God the Father loves to shine the light of his glory on the person of Jesus, the Son of God. In fact, at the baptism of Christ, the heavens opened and God turned the spotlight up bright upon his Son.

> When Jesus was baptized, he immediately came up out of the water. Heaven was opened to him, and he saw the Spirit of God coming down like a dove and resting on him. A voice from heaven said, "This is my Son whom I dearly love; I find happiness in him." (Matt 3:16-17 CEB)

In this moment, God the Father was honoring God the Son. It was a joyful moment; one not to be missed. Herein we are given a peek inside the ultimate honoring circle, the Divine Team. But, there are a few other privileged moments not to be missed, as well.

The Spotlight Scriptures

In a similar manner, and on another occasion, the subject arose about the good works that Jesus had been able to accomplish. As soon as they were mentioned to him, however, something surprising happened. He immediately took out a spotlight of his own and shone it on someone else. See if you can spot it:

> Jesus responded to the Jewish leaders, "I assure you that the Son can't do anything by himself except what he sees the Father doing. Whatever the Father does, the Son does likewise. The Father loves the Son and shows him everything that he does. He will show him greater works than these so that you will marvel. As the Father raises the dead and gives life, so too does the Son give life to whomever he wishes. The Father doesn't judge anyone, but he has given all judgment to the Son so that everyone will honor the Son just as they honor the Father. Whoever doesn't honor the Son doesn't honor the Father who sent him. (John 5:19-23 CEB)

In this instance of affirmation, Jesus immediately defers the honor to his Father, shining the spotlight straightly and swiftly on him. "I assure you that the Son can't do anything by himself except what he sees the Father doing" (v. 19a). Once again, Jesus turns to the Divine Team and shares the glory.

Perhaps most fascinating of these spotlight scriptures is the time shortly before Jesus' arrest and crucifixion when he is preparing his disciples for the challenging times they would soon face. He informs them that he is going to be leaving, but another member of the Divine Team will be coming:

> If you love me, you will keep my commandments. I will ask the Father, and he will send another Companion, who will be with you forever. This Companion is the Spirit of Truth, whom the world can't receive because it neither sees him nor recognizes him. You know him, because he lives with you and will be with you. (John 14:15-17 CEB)

True to form, Jesus introduces another member of the Divine Team. He shines the light on the Spirit of God, honoring the person and relational role ("Companion" or "Comforter") that he will fill in the lives of the disciples.

But he does something more. Perhaps something that even more so reveals how much a value the act of honoring is within the Godhead. Look at how Jesus describes the Holy Spirit, how he helps the disciples to know it is him when he appears:

> But when the Friend comes, the Spirit of the Truth, he will take you by the hand and guide you into all the truth there is. *He won't draw attention to himself,* but will make sense out of what is about to happen and, indeed, out of all that I have done and said. *He will honor me;* he will

take from me and deliver it to you. (John 16:12-14 THE MESSAGE, italics mine)

Did you catch it? In essence, Jesus was shining the spotlight on the Holy Spirit, honoring him and, then, telling his disciples how they will know when the Spirit arrives. Jesus says that the Spirit will not speak about himself but will remind them about Jesus and all that he has taught them. In other words, when the Spirit comes, here's how you will know it is him: he won't be talking about himself, but will be holding a big spotlight and shining it on Jesus and on his words. The Spirit is another member of the Divine Team, the Ultimate Honoring Circle.

The doctrine of the Trinity, then, is not merely some transcendent and lofty truth tucked away on the top shelf of theology; it is vibrant and practical and exemplary to our experience of faith today. It reveals much about God's life with us and our lives with one another.

A true teaming culture not only accomplishes things God wants done, it also reflects who God is. This is the primary distinctive of a true ministry team. It can be said that God, or the Godhead, dwells in community. The Trinity is, in fact, a community or communion of Persons. The Trinity, then, is the Divine Team—the one we should seek to emulate and follow in our faith communities, families, and teams.

The Trinity as Divine Community

The foremost metaphor or model for teams in the Bible is the Trinity. According to Stanley Grentz, Trinitarian thinking has emerged in recent history to become "one of the most widely acknowledged Christian teachings."[1] He also notes, "The doctrine of the Trinity is not ultimately a teaching about 'God' but a teaching about *God's life with us and our life with each other*. It is the life of communion and indwelling, God in us, all of us in each other."[2]

In a mysterious sense, the Bible reveals God as a collaborator. Within the three persons of the Trinity and their interrelationships, we see a constant flow of communication and collaboration, even celebration. This has intrigued and perplexed theologians for centuries. Our opportunity in the church, however, is to emulate and reflect this Divine Community on our teams and within our small groups.

The Teaming God?

The interactions of the members of the Trinity reveal an honoring circle, the utmost example for today's ministry teams. Andy Stanley and

Bill Willits note a number of honoring and engaging activities among the members of the Divine Team, including:

> The Trinity—God the Father, Son, and Spirit—is seen expressing a unique, affirming kind of relationship toward one another. They are seen enjoying one another (Gen. 1:26), encouraging one another (Mt. 3:17), supporting one another (John 14:25), loving one another (Mk. 9:7), deferring to one another (John 14:10), and glorifying one another (John 17:1).[3]

It can be said that God, or the Godhead, dwells in community. Stanley Grenz has said, "The very doctrine of the Trinity is based on a relational God living in community both within and without."[4] The Trinity is a community or communion of Persons. The life and workings of the Trinity, then, may be considered as an image of teaming and teamwork. God has chosen to carry out his work through not just one, but through all three Persons of the Trinity.

> The Bible paints many marvelous images of team life. For the ultimate picture of a ministry team, we need look no further than the Trinity: the Father, Son, and the Holy Spirit. The members of the Trinity share a common vision for ministry. They enjoy fellowship in wonderfully loving relationships. And each member of the Trinity has a unique "task" or role in the process known as salvation history. They are the essential fusion of relationships and work—the missional fellowship.[5]

Teaming Characteristics within the Trinity

Among the characteristics of the Trinity that best convey their life as the Divine Team are:

- creativity;
- collaboration;
- community;
- cooperation;
- communication, and
- humility.

The ultimate creative act was creation itself. And, creation was a collaborative effort. Remember, the seven days of creation were not implemented by a "me" but by an "us." Collaboration is seen in the expressions of the Godhead from the earliest accounts of Genesis and is evidenced within the Trinity. For God says, "Let *us* make human beings in *our* image, to be like *us*" (Gen 1:26a NLT, italics mine). In the very words that spoke the worlds into order, the words of God are more than singular statements or affirmations; upon closer examination, they are the running dialogue of a team of Persons. Stanley Grentz wrote, "Creation . . . is a trinitarian act. It is the result of the working together of all three persons of the eternal Trinity. . . . The Father *creates* the world, *through* the Son, *by* his Spirit."[6]

God not only calls his church, and the various teams and communities that form it, to function in collaboration, he also calls them to practice and experience biblical community. Not only has God destined Christ-followers to experience community, God himself dwells *in* community; He is a community of Persons. It is the culture of the Divine. The Trinity is a community or communion of Persons. This doctrine was established in the church by the end of the fourth century and became known as the *perichoretic union.*

At its core, the concept of the perichoretic union is a circle dance. The image understood by the early church fathers most befitting the nature of the Trinity was of a celebratory dance. What a beautiful image for teams. Think of the dancing and celebrating among the Jewish families in *Fiddler on the Roof,* and you may have a hint of what this refers to. The Trinity is a celebration of persons and of joy. The great news is that teams within the church have the potential to be the same.

> The LORD your God is with you.
>   He is a hero who saves you.
>   He happily rejoices over you,
>   renews you with his love,
>   and celebrates over you with shouts of joy.
> (Zeph 3:17 *GOD'S WORD*)

The life, workings, and activities of the Trinity, then, may be considered as an image of teaming and teamwork. God has chosen to carry out his work not just through one, but through all three Persons of the Trinity.

Cooperation is another teaming characteristic exemplified by the three Persons of the Trinity. The workings of each member represented in the biblical account reveals a consistent teaming nature to their work or getting the work done together. It is not uncommon for Christians to assign separate and distinct components of the work of God to each of the three Persons of the Trinity. However, a more accurate theological description of their roles would be to say that each member of the Trinity works together in cooperation on divine initiatives beginning in the biblical record with the work of creation. Although we cite Jesus as the member of the Trinity who hung on the cross and was resurrected, it is also true that "in him dwelleth all the fullness of the Godhead bodily" (Col 2:9 KJV).

Another teaming component that exists in the Trinity is communication. This is seen in several instances in the Gospels. Shortly before Jesus' crucifixion, for instance, in the moments of final discourse with his team of disciples, Jesus communicates with his team and tries to prepare them by helping them understand what is coming. He said that he was going away but that he would "not leave [them] as orphaned" (John 14:18a). He promises that the Father would send "the Comforter," or "the Counselor, the Holy Spirit." He even says that when the Father sends the Holy Spirit, he will send him in Jesus' name. Clearly, we see the three members of the Trinity collaborating and honoring the other members constantly. The collaboration, cooperation, and communication among the members of the Trinity are so prevalent and organic that this community is wholly unified and can be described as the ultimate expression of relational oneness. So much so that Jesus said, "I and the Father are one" and "I am in the Father and the Father is in me" (John 10:30; 14:9, 11; 17:11, 21 NIV).

The Most Unexpected Characteristic

Perhaps the most surprising of all the characteristics of the members of the Trinity is humility. After all, conventional wisdom may suggest that a deity is to be worshiped and it is subjects alone that must express humility. Not so, however, in the Christian tradition.

There is something Jesus says about the Spirit during his earthly ministry that seems to convey the most unexpected characteristic one would propose to find in a deity and that is self-humiliation or selflessness. Jesus says that when the Spirit comes "He will not speak on His own initiative, but whatever He hears, He will speak" (John 16:13 NASB). On another occasion Jesus acknowledged that he avoided the temptations of independence (John 7:1-4) and, rather, conveyed his own interdependence when he said,

> My teaching is not my own. It comes from him who sent me. If anyone chooses to do God's will, he will find out whether my teaching comes from God or whether I speak on my own. He who speaks on his own does so to gain *honor for himself,* but he who works for the *honor of the one who sent him* is a man of truth; there is nothing false about him. (7:16-18 NIV, italics mine)

Jesus embodied the characteristic of selflessness and absolute humility as has no other man on the planet. On one occasion, he said, "If I glorify myself, my glory means nothing. My Father, whom you claim as your God, is the one who glorifies me" (John 8:54 NIV).

The Teaming Church Principle #4: A Collaborative Community

Great teaming leaders are not only people developers, they are also community architects. The true teaming leader is aware of his or her environment and of how key values shape it. The role of culture is vital to the development of a teaming church. The culture of which I speak represents the right kind of environment the team needs in order to endure and thrive—one that reflects the relationship of the Trinity, a collaborative environment. It is teaming essential #4: "To become a great team your group must have a deeply challenging goal, a creatively empowering leader, and a *collaborative*, biblically honoring *community*."

Another Fatal Team Error

One mistake that will cause a team to wither or simply fall apart is if it has a culture that is overly controlled. Granted, teams need some structure, but they also need free spaces to imagine, think, dream, and develop. Great team leaders have the opportunity to shape the culture around them.

To review and move ahead a step further, here are the teaming errors:

Fatal Teaming Error #1: When a team is undervalued.
Fatal Teaming Error #2: When a team is underchallenged.
Fatal Teaming Error #3: A leader who holds onto power.
Fatal Teaming Error #4: A culture that is overly controlled.

Some important questions for a teaming leader to ask about culture are: What are the driving values that shape our team culture in the church? Is our sense of teaming culture growing stronger or weaker? Who are the key influencers of our teaming culture? What could we do to strengthen our teaming environment? What are some of the best stories we have to tell of teams and teaming accomplishments and relationships?

A church culture is overly controlled when:

- Most leadership roles stay the same for several years at a time.
- It takes a long time to get a decision made.
- Communication within the church moves slowly.

Great collaborations in a church and on its ministry teams come from training and strong interest. The team leader is the one who is primarily responsible for cultivating a community that is truly collaborative.

The Circle Dance

The relationship that exists between the members of the Trinity holds more than mere organizational significance. God doesn't just do community; he is communal and relational by his very nature. That is to say, the relationship is not contrived. It is more like a flowing dance than a rigid organizational model.

In his book, *Leading the Team-Based Church*, George Cladis further describes the perichoretic union:

> *Perichoresis* means literally "circle dance." *Choros* in ancient Greek referred to a round dance performed at banquets and festive occasions. . . .
> Based on the biblical descriptions of Father, Son and Spirit, John [of Damascus] depicted the three persons of the Trinity in a circle. A *perichoretic* image of the Trinity is that of the three persons of God in constant movement in a circle that implies intimacy, equality, unity, and yet distinction among the various members and love.
> Theologian Shirley Guthrie calls this image of God a "lovely picture that portrays the persons of the Trinity in a kind of choreography" (Greek *choros-graphy*), similar to ballet. In this circle dance of God is a sense of joy, freedom, song, intimacy, and harmony. "The oneness of God is not the oneness of a distinct, self-contained individual; it is the unity of a *community* of persons who love each other and live together in harmony."[7]

The Trinity emerges as the highest and most essential biblical model for effective teambuilding. Every other model is but a reflection of this central one. The Trinity is such a transcendent and mysterious theme that Augustine spent thirty years writing a fifteen-book treatise on the subject. Jonathan Edwards considered it such a key theme in Scripture that among all biblical truths he referred to it as the "Supreme Harmony of All."[8] And, Stanley Grenz cites, "the doctrine of the Trinity forms the foundation for the Christian conception of the essence of God."[9]

This transcendent model of the Trinitarian relationship, though not wholly reproducible, may be reflected within humanity in various communitarian interactions such as marriage, family, Christian fellowship, and ministry teams and partnerships. In other words, in the same sense in which humans are made in the image of God not in order to reproduce or replicate God's likeness, but rather to reflect and represent it on earth, so ministry teams can be a reflection of the Trinity, or the Divine Community and their collaborations. They are a part of the reflections of God's glory in the earth.

The More Important Question

The essential question that must be considered as it relates to the Trinity and using it as the ultimate model for ministry teams, however, is not whether the doctrine of the Trinity is relevant to humanity or to the church; rather, it is this: *Is humanity and the church relevant to the Trinity and to this doctrine?* Stated differently, the most important consideration is not, what will this doctrine do for any individual Christian or particular local church, but, rather, in light of this revelation, how should we conduct ourselves as Christians, as church leaders, and as collaborative teams in ministry?

After these considerations, it seems then that the circle dance image of the Trinity cited by John of Damascus, and affirmed by Cladis, among others, is a vibrant model for teambuilding in the twenty-first century. On one dimension, it is encouraging to rediscover a model of ministry that can provide practical application and amplification to the essential doctrine of the Trinity, something all too rare in modern Christianity. The Trinity is the premier model, or the master image, of what Christian fellowship, community, and teamwork are to look like for the purposes of edification, evangelization, and, ultimately, the glorification of God on earth.

Reflecting the Trinity on a Team

A closer look at the Trinity as a model reveals powerful principles for today's ministry teams. Although these traits are divine in origin, they are clearly the qualities that enrich human relationships that inspire us to grow in Christ and deepen our relationships. These practices cause teaming efforts to flourish. They bring out the glory of God in our communities of faith.

But, just how can a team reflect the nature and glory of God, the Trinity?

First, the divine love that exists between the members of the Godhead is best described, and defined, as "self-giving."

The members of the Trinity constantly convey a sense of humility, honor, and service to one another. The divine love that holds them together also compels their unending service to one another.

Interestingly enough, Jesus also taught his followers that the only way to find their lives would be by emulating this self-giving practice displayed within the Trinity: "If you try to hang on to your life, you will lose it. But if you give up your life for my sake and for the sake of the Good News, you will save it" (Mark 8:35 NLT).

Dallas Willard challenges us to not only have the right information about the Trinity but also to let our belief in it revolutionize our relationships:

> Nearly every professing Christian has some information about the Trinity, the incarnation, the atonement, and other standard doctrines. But to have the "right" answers about the Trinity, for example, and to actually *believe* in the reality of the Trinity, is all the difference in the world.
>
> The advantage of believing in the reality of the Trinity is not that we get an A from God for giving "the right answer." Remember, to believe something is to act as if it is so . . . the advantage of believing in the Trinity is that we then live as if the Trinity is real: as if the cosmos environing us actually is, beyond all else, a self-sufficing community of unspeakably magnificent personal beings of boundless love, knowledge, and power. And, thus believing, our lives naturally integrate themselves, through our actions, into the reality of such a universe, just as with two plus two equals four. [10]

Second, a church that worships and serves in community reflects and becomes the image of God within society.

The *Imago Dei* is not only something humankind is born with, but also something that gives us the potential to represent God on earth through community. Our observations of the relationships that exist among the members of the Trinity provide powerful insight into how God wants us to relate to one another in community. Living in the image of God is no isolated discipline; it is a sacrament of community.

John Champion sums it up well:

> Where did man get his social nature, if not from his image of, and likeness to, God? In man or in God, personality cannot be personality apart and alone. As has often been said, "God as One Person is no Person." If He were but One Person, He would be shut up within Himself to live a lifeless life, devoid of personal interest, intercourse and content. In one way a self-existent life is a contradiction in terms. Life must be correspondent: it must be reciprocity. [11]

Third, community is not an optional or extracurricular activity for the believer; it is the context in which God has chosen to reveal himself.

Relationship is central to God's plan for the life of every Christian. It is the context in which God dwells and the one into which he calls us to dwell. While sin fragments and disrupts community, righteousness and justice heal, mend, and create community and communities. Bilezikian sizes up the paramount importance of community in a clear and convincing manner:

> Community as God ordained it was not an incidental concern of [God's] nor did it happen haphazardly. . . . Community is deeply grounded in the nature of God. It flows from who God is. Because he is community, he creates community. It is his gift of himself to humans.
>
> Therefore, the making of community may not be regarded as an optional decision for Christians. It is a compelling and irrevocable necessity, a binding mandate for all believers at all times. It is possible for humans to reject or alter God's commission for them to build community and to be in community. But this may happen only at the cost of forsaking the Creator of community and of betraying his image in us; this cost is enormous, since his image in us is the essential attribute that defines our own humanity. [12]

Teaming, then, not only is the preferred method for getting the work of the Church accomplished, it also does something deeper in the heart of the Christ-follower. It becomes a prime opportunity to glorify God and to come closer to reflecting the image of God amidst our experiences of community and collaboration. As "two or three come together" in his name, in some powerful and mysterious way, he is there in the midst. Something of God, the Trinity, is reflected within the team. And, God is pleased.

But, what are some of the other powerful metaphors and pictures in the Bible that will help us better understand the role and function of ministry teams? There are more than a few.

A Teaming Leader Interview, Mega-church: Rod Loy

Rod Loy, lead pastor, First Assembly, North Little Rock, Arkansas, www.firstnlr. com

Q: How long have you pastored this church?

A: Ten-and-a half years.

Q: What is your average weekly attendance currently?

A: 3,678.

Q: How important and integral are teams and teambuilding to your church? What role have they played throughout its history so far and what role do they play today?

A: Teams are key. We organize and lead by utilizing short-term teams. The teams exist for the duration of the initiative or event and then are disbanded. The only standing team is our creative team, working on Sunday services. One unique thing we do is, the leader of the team is selected and then given draft picks. They get to live draft a specified number of people to serve with them. That way, they can organize their team from inside or outside the staff by gift mix, personality, and so on, as they see fit. The team is autonomous. It reports and gives recommendations at the end of the process, or in many cases has budget and approval authority to accomplish the goal. Every team is slightly different. I do not lead any team. We've learned that the leader in charge contributes to groupthink and diminishes the effectiveness of the team.

Q: What would you say makes for a great ministry team? What characterizes it?

A: A great ministry team is made up of different personalities, giftings, energy, age, and so on, with all of them organized around or buying into a common goal. The more diverse the team, the better its opportunity to be great.

Q: What characterizes the most effective team players at your church? What does it take to be a great team player?

A: Most effective team players are those who are able to express differing opinions without anger or unhealthy emotional engagement. We've done a lot of teaching on interaction between team members. Great team players understand their differing opinions are precisely why they are on the team.

Q: How important is a great goal to a great team?

A: That's kind of a "what came first, the chicken or the egg" question. A great team can determine the parameters of the goal. Often in churches what we form are solution-finding groups, tasked with coming to a conclusion as opposed to presenting the team with a problem or challenge and allowing them to determine the goal. It might be semantics, but I like to let the team determine specific goals. I want to provide broad direction.

Q: What have you come to understand about teams and team leadership today?

A: Most churches know the language of teams. Very few churches actually function as teams. All the language can be deceptive, making you think true teamwork is actually happening. In fact, working as teams, with leadership shifting with the situation, context, goal, and assignment is a rare thing.

Q: What are some essential practices and values of great team leaders?

A: (1) They don't offer their ideas first; (2) they don't immediately react to good or bad ideas; (3) they value differing opinions and approaches; (4) they are flexible in approach; (5) they know how to put the right people on their team, for instance knowing the importance of both dreamers and planners; and (6) they are loyal to the leader and the organization.

Q: What are some of the best questions you have ever asked your team?

A: There are several:

- What if we were told we couldn't have church next Sunday, or ever again. What would we do?

- If we had never seen a church service, what would the components be?

- If we could start over from the beginning, what would we do different? What would we eliminate?

- Are we too big? Do we need to find a way to restrict further growth until we are producing fully formed followers?

- Do we focus too much on innovation? Should we be more content with duplication? Why? Why not?

- How could I change to help our church be more healthy?

Drawing Your Circle

Questions to Ask Your Team

1. In what ways does a ministry team reflect the nature of God and of the Trinity? How is that significant to ministry?

2. How does your team reflect the creativity of God?

3. How does your team reflect the community of God?

4. In what ways do your communications as a team reflect the nature of God?

5. Does your team ever exhibit a collective humility? How so?

6. What are some times when you felt you have been too controlling as a team leader?

Chapter Nine

Teaming Models and Metaphors: The Images That Help Us Draw Better Circles

People are moving from literacy to visual-cy.
—*Andy Crouch,* Culture-Making

Effective teaming leaders not only draw great circles, they also paint vivid full-color pictures of what teams can become. Metaphors, models, or word pictures are vital tools in a teaming leader's toolbox. Just think of the word pictures Jesus used with his own circle, the disciples, as he sought to describe what they could (and would) become:

- the vine and the branches;
- the salt of the earth;
- the light of the world;
- a city set upon a hill;
- the sheep of his pasture; and
- family ("my brothers and my mother").

In order to motivate, prepare, and develop his followers, Jesus frequently used models and metaphors. Visual language was important then and it still is today. Teams need models; if people can see (or picture) a great team, they just may be able to become one.

According to cultural analyst Andy Crouch:

> Many centuries after the shift from oral to written culture, we are now well along in the transition to [a] visual culture—where the predominant mode of communication is images rather than words. Just as the shift to writing required the skills we call literacy, so visual culture requires its own skills—for lack of a better word, visualcy.[1]

Models Reveal Mystery

Careful consideration must be paid not only to the message we bring as church leaders but also the methods and models of equipping people for ministry. But, just what is meant by the term "models"? Harold Snyder's book, *Models of the Kingdom,* says a model is "a useful methodology for clarifying theological issues."[2] In other words, a model is an illustrative representation of a principle, insight, or truth. It helps to make truth plain and vivid. Snyder says, "[A model] is a somewhat formalized way of using metaphorical language to describe or to explore some reality not fully understood. . . . In this sense, models help to reveal mystery."

What are the most powerful biblical images of a great ministry team? And, how can team leaders and members best use these metaphors and models to inspire and lead their teams? There are a number of biblical images that form great motivating models for ministry teams. Among them are: the family, the three-fold chord of Ecclesiastes, the twelve disciples of Jesus, the Triumvirate, and Paul's vision in First Corinthians of the church as a human body. Each of these is worth considering as an image for teams and teambuilding.

Teaming Model #1: Marriage and Children—The Circle of Family

The first human team God formed on earth was the circle of a family. Larry Richards writes, "The family is viewed in both testaments as a basic unit of the believing community. In the New Testament the image of the family is one of the primary ways in which scripture explains the nature of Christians' relationship with God and one another."[3]

The image of family is woven throughout the New Testament. Clearly the apostle Paul and others saw it as a powerful example and fluid expression to help believers imagine and understand their relationship to God and to one another. Christ-followers are addressed repeatedly as brothers and sisters. Also, the church is characterized as the "household of God":

> So now you are no longer strangers and aliens. Rather, you are fellow citizens with God's people, and *you belong to God's household*. As God's household, you are built on the foundation of the apostles and prophets with Christ Jesus himself as the cornerstone. (Eph 2:19-20 CEB, italics mine)

Paul also draws on the family as a type of proving grounds for leadership in the church. "They should manage their own household well—they should see that their children are obedient with complete respect, because if they don't know how to manage their own household, how can they take care of God's church?" (1 Tim 3:4-5 CEB).

Paul says that before you propose to draw circles of church (or church teams), it is important that you show your faithfulness by drawing your family circle. Diligence and attention to the smaller circles of life are what qualify us to oversee the larger ones. Leadership in the church is similar to leadership in the home.

God's observation after watching Adam's first efforts at a solo-flight existence in the garden of Eden was, "It is not good for the man to be alone" (Gen 2:18a NLT). In God's estimation, man unquestionably needed a partner, a collaborator, a completer, and a companion: "I will make a helper who is just right for him" (Gen 2:18b NLT). After observing the earliest efforts of man at independent governance within the garden, the Godhead came to one conclusion: man needed help or, to use KJV language, a "help-meet"! Not only did God form a woman in the garden, he also formed a team—the first one, in fact. Eventually his world would be filled with such teams or partnerships. God wanted a planet covered with them.

Scripture says, "This explains why a man leaves his father and mother and is joined to his wife, and the two are united into one" (Gen 2:24 NLT). In other words, to incorporate the preferred model and to paraphrase: "This is why a man will eventually want to leave his family circle of origin and form a circle of his own." When we enter this planet we are born into a team, or a potential one, at least. We are nurtured in the circle of family and we mature with a desire to form a circle or team of our own. Although this is not always the case, such as in instances of celibacy, it is nonetheless arguably the order and design of God in the biblical record. Generally speaking, people cannot thrive alone and certainly cannot reproduce alone. We are designed to emerge in life amidst a team, amidst a circle comprised of meaningful and supportive relationships.

Consider this insight from Gilbert Bilezikian, a man who has served as a founding elder and theological advisor to Bill Hybels and Willow Creek Community Church, which currently numbers some twenty thousand in worship on a weekend:

> The biblical metaphor of "family" more appropriately describes what the church should resemble—a group of people, few enough in numbers to sit around in a circle, facing each other and sharing the joy and the benefits of togetherness. Every church that aspires to function as community must make a small group structure available to its constituency. The alternative is to shrink to the status of a Sunday morning worship station. A congregation that comprises more than fifty adults is too large to function as community—unless it is organized in small groups where communal life can thrive.[4]

A team is a family.

Teaming Model #2: The Three-Fold Cord: The Circle of Camaraderie

The biblical value of teams over individual efforts is described in resonant and simple terms in the book of Ecclesiastes. It is especially interesting that, although he held a supreme hierarchical position, the book's writer, King Solomon, nonetheless saw the wisdom and value of teams even in his day. Even from his lofty throne he thought to include these insights and the model of the triple-braided cord in his volume of wisdom.

> Two people are better off than one, for they can help each other succeed. If one person falls, the other can reach out and help. But someone who falls alone is in real trouble. Likewise, two people lying close together can keep each other warm. But how can one be warm alone? A person standing alone can be attacked and defeated, but two can stand back-to-back and conquer. Three are even better, for a triple-braided cord is not easily broken. (Eccl 4:9-12 NLT)

This text is used most often, perhaps, at weddings, but is frequently taken out of context. Traditionally, many Bible teachers have sentimentally assumed and conveyed that the three-fold chord represents the union of husband and wife enjoined with the presence of God. Although such exposition may comprise an appropriate, beautiful, and even biblical, image, it does not pass the exegetical test, nor does it convey the context of the passage. When considering the verses that fall just prior to this passage, the contrasting introduction makes it clear that the purpose of this image in Scripture is not to present the need for a relationship with God, nor to provide an incentive to marry, but to emphasize the importance of human collaboration amidst our work or vocation as opposed to individualism or isolation.

Consider the preface to the familiar passage:

> Again I saw something meaningless under the sun:
>
> There was a man all alone;
>   he had neither son nor brother.
> There was no end to his toil,
>   yet his eyes were not content with his wealth.
> "For whom am I toiling," he asked,
>   "and why am I depriving myself of enjoyment?"
> This too is meaningless—
>   a miserable business! (Eccl 4:7-8 NIV)

These words set the stage for Solomon's triple-braided cord teaming image. He presents the problem of individualistic efforts and expresses the futility of "a man all alone" who "works to gain as much wealth as he can." The results are that, even though he may experience some success, he has no one with whom to share it. Thus, in the final analysis, he concludes that "it is all so meaningless and depressing." He finds himself right back where Adam was in the garden—alone. The place that God said is "not good."

Solomon cites several specific benefits of the three-fold team or group, over individual efforts, including greater productivity—"[they] are better off than one"; greater results—"help each other succeed"; and greater security—"if one person falls, the other can . . . help" and "two can stand back-to-back and conquer." He also notes that the addition of another team member is an even greater benefit—"three are even better."

A team is a strong union.

Teaming Model #3: The Twelve: The Circle of Ministry

When Jesus arrived as the Messiah, he confounded the expectations of everyone. The scribes, the Pharisees, the people, even the disciples, expected the Messiah to come in great display of power to form an instant pyramid or triangle of self-sustaining and self-centered force. They just knew he would establish an immediate hierarchy and assume a throne. Instead he took on the form of a servant (Phil 2:5-11) and invested himself primarily into the work of forming a team.

In a figurative sense, Jesus was more interested in drawing circles than triangles. He came drawing a circle of comrades, a circle not only of collaboration, discipleship, and mentoring in the chosen twelve but also surprising to many, even a circle of friends (John 15:15). Bill Hybels describes his leadership this way:

> Jesus . . . provides us a model of a leader who built a cohesive, loving team. One incident toward the end of his life is particularly touching. On the eve of his betrayal, he gathered his team together in the Upper Room and drew them close with these words: "I earnestly desire to share this meal with you." Then he broke the bread and shared the wine. His instructions for the future were specific. They were to continue this practice of remembering him, *in community.* Think of it. The first time communion was ever taken it was a team experience. And it's supposed to continue to be a team experience.[5]

Although much weight has been placed upon the words of Christ, it is important that we also lend weight to his ways, his chosen strategies, and tactics. They, of course, are also inspired, and a powerful model for the way we live out our faith. It is important to consider not only what he said to the Twelve but also to consider how he called, equipped, instructed, and mobilized them for ministry. The words of Christ are important, but so are his ways.

> Jesus himself was teamwork-obsessed. He spent his ministry not founding local communities or growing a mega-following for himself, but building a handful of itinerant disciples in first-century Palestine into a great team that could create a culture of perichoretic love. He called out his disciples in many cases in teams. He sent out his disciples always in teams. [6]

A team is a group of disciples.

Teaming Model/Metaphor #4: The Triumvirate—The Circle of Responsibility

Not only did Jesus build a team of disciples; he also built a team within a team. This was Jesus' inner circle, called the Triumvirate by theologians. It could be argued that by his investment in them he built a team of teambuilders. This inner circle of disciples consisted of Peter, James, and John.

The Triumvirate, according to the biblical account, was closer to Jesus than the rest of the Twelve. They saw more, heard more, and experienced more. Jesus seemed to confide in these three more than the rest, allowing them to share in his pain at the garden of Gethsemane (Matt 26:35-37; Mark 14:31-33) and in his glory at the Mount of Transfiguration (Matt 17:1-3; Mark 9:1-3) on a unique level.

Ultimately, these three would be given greater responsibility than the rest. Peter would be called to oversee the church among the Jewish believers. James would be called to pastor the church at Jerusalem. John would be the trusted teacher of Jesus' words, the scribe of a Gospel account, and the privileged conduit of the Revelation of Jesus Christ. Much was ultimately required of this team in service to God; and, accordingly, the Son of God also invested much in them.

The Triumvirate reflected the master image of the Trinity in that they were joined together by a common relationship and cause. Each of them was conjoined into the group or team not because of similar vocation or similar temperament, but by a common relationship and calling. Each of the three had a higher calling that was initiated by their introduction to Jesus. This quality of oneness exhibited in the Trinity would be the goal of Christ for these three men and the other disciples, as well. Jesus clearly prayed that the oneness expressed in their interrelatedness would reflect that of the Trinity.

A team is a privileged, and responsible few.

Teaming Model/Metaphor #5: The Body of Christ (Paul's Vision): The Circle of Interdependence

The New Testament portrays the church (*ekklesia*) as a "body" on three occasions—in Romans 12; 1 Corinthians 12; and Ephesians 4. On each occurrence a set of common values are presented, including interdependence, solidarity, spiritual gifts, and love. In 1 Corinthians 12:12–27, Paul presents this team model in vivid detail by offering the conflicted Corinthian church a vivid image of the *ekklesia* in the form of a human body. This model presents a church that is more than an organization, but rather an organism, an organic and living being sustained by the work of the Holy Spirit through a variety of bodily systems. Paul's description includes a clear image common to each believer—and even to pagans—for the human body. Throughout this passage, a few key principles emerge that are important to effective teambuilding or bodybuilding within the local church.

First, the church is a place of diversity in that it is one body made up of many parts with varied gifts and from varied backgrounds. Second, unity is a characteristic in that one Spirit who is within us all unites Christians. Third, solidarity is a characteristic since separation from the body of any part is unthinkable.

The principles continue to unfold in this passage. Fourth, value is seen in that each function and gift is uniquely important to the overall body. Fifth, interdependence is a key characteristic in that we need one another. Sixth, harmony is revealed in that those parts of the body that appear to be the weakest are the most necessary. Seventh, intimacy is also a part in that an individual success is a team success and an individual suffering is a team suffering. And eighth, support is shown in that one member's strength offset another's weakness.

Paul also exhibited a commitment to consistent collaboration with his many partners in ministry. This was even shown by the terms he used to refer to them, including: "fellow labourers" (Phil 4:3; 1 Thess 3:2), "fellow helpers" (2 Cor 8:23; 3 John 8), "fellow servants" (Col 1:7; 4:7), "fellow soldiers" (Phil 2:25), "fellow workers" (Col 4:11), and even "yoke fellow" (Phil 4:3 KJV).

Rick Warren has said, "The church is a body, not a business. It is an organism, not an organization! It is a family to be loved, not a machine to be engineered, and not a company to be managed."

The image of the local church and its ministry teams as a body provides a model that is always relevant, since we are all physical creatures. Also, it provides a model that is more organic in nature, and represents a network of cooperative systems.

A team is a body.

Motivating Models

These models of teams and community are powerful tools for today's pastor and church leader. Painting vivid pictures of the church unified and flowing together in ministry gives the Holy Spirit tools to inspire servant leaders.

Models, images, metaphors, and stories are powerful sources of inspiration to teams. Have you noticed how everyone in the congregation sits up and pays a little closer attention when the pastor's sermon moves from text to story? The moment he or she interjects something personal into the monologue, a part of the congregational mind ignites. Vital neurons light up and souls are engaged. It is when truth becomes incarnate in life. Models and images in the Bible have the same effect.

A few places that teams and teaming leaders can use these metaphors and models are:

1. In a sermon series. A sermon (or series) that is tied to a vivid metaphor is more memorable.

2. Teaching a small-group study or Sunday school class.

3. In e-mails, texts, and communiques to your team members.

4. For ideas in choosing names for your team or ministry.

Teaming leaders always look for stories, examples, biblical insights, and images to help inspire, challenge, and motivate their teams and team members. Remember, models reveal mysteries. They not only open up the Word of God to people, they also open up a world of opportunities to serve others.

God wants your team to be strong. He wants your team to be effective. He wants your team to thrive. But, how can you tell if your team is truly thriving?

A Teaming Leader Interview, Multi-Campus Church: Craig Groeschel

Craig Groeschel, lead pastor, LifeChurch.tv, Oklahoma City, and thirteen other campuses to date

Q: How important and integral are teams and teambuilding to LifeChurch? What role have they played throughout its history and what role do they play today?

A: Building teams is one of the most important things that we do. In the early days of the church, we were building teams before we even knew to call it "building teams." We were just working on gathering groups of people to work on a common mission. Teambuilding is essential in everything we do to fulfill our mission "to lead people to become fully devoted followers of Christ."

Q: What would you say makes for a great ministry team? What characterizes it?

A: A great team is a collection of great people with different gifts but the same mission.

Q: What characterizes the most effective team players at Life-Church? What does it take to be a great team player?

A: One thing that always makes a great team is having very defined values because what we value determines what we do. We build our teams around values. We actually define specific behavioral values. We looked at all of the most significant team players and asked, "What values do they have in common?" We found things like teachability, flexibility, work ethic, and others. What does it take? It takes an understanding of your strengths and your weaknesses and your contribution to the overall goal and the overall mission.

Q: How important is a great goal to a great team?

A: More than a great goal, I'd say having a great mission is important. For us, we don't try to create long-term goals; we create short-term, achievable goals. Sometimes when a goal is met, there is a letdown in work ethic, efficiency, or effectiveness; so instead of being goal driven, we try to be mission driven. Our different teams create their own goals underneath the overarching mission of the organization.

Q: What have you come to understand about teams and team leadership today that you did not know fifteen years ago?

A: Our vocabulary of working with teams has grown. Fifteen years ago, we were dealing with fewer people and had fewer teams. What I've learned is to have one big team of smaller teams that each have their own projects underneath the global mission.

Q: What are some essential practices and values for being a great team leader?

A: A few things. One is we have to be a developer of people, to see potential in people, and help bring it out. We have to be willing to have transparent conversations. At the same time, we need to be team players as leaders. We are not just coaches but player-coaches. We need to remain teachable and keep growing, so our players don't outgrow us.

Q: What theology would you say motivates or informs your practice of using and developing ministry teams?

A: Unquestionably Jesus gathering the twelve disciples to train and release them into the world to do his mission.

Q: Have the ingredients of a great ministry team at LifeChurch changed as the church has grown? In other words, do the things that constitute a great team in a megachurch differ at all from those

that constitute a great team in a small- or medium-sized church? Explain.

A: The principles of team don't change based on the size. The only difference is we are one big team of many smaller teams.

Drawing Your Circle

Questions to Ask Your Team

1. The quote by Andy Crouch at the start of the chapter says that our society is moving from "literacy to visual-cy"? In what ways do you see this occurring? How should that reality affect our work, our training, and our ministry?

2. In what ways is a ministry team like "the salt of the earth"?

3. In what ways is a church or ministry team "a city set upon a hill"?

4. In what ways is a church or ministry team "the sheep of his pasture"?

5. In what ways is a church or ministry team "a family"?

6. In what ways is a church or ministry team "a body"?

Chapter Ten

Creating Circles Where People Can Thrive: A Teaming Culture

This generation loves big dreams, but they are tired
of those that come up short.
They need to see how to get there.
—*Bobby Gruenewald, founder of YouVersion.com and the Bible App*

The larger a church gets, the more imperative it
becomes for its leaders to minister within a team
culture instead of as solo practitioners.
—*George Barna*

Teaming churches refresh their teams and team members frequently. The process of moving from one or two strong teams to a churchwide teaming culture requires intention and dedication. It takes determination and inspiration to cultivate thriving teams, and it takes the same elements to keep them thriving.

Left to itself, a team will always drift into some state of ineffectiveness. If the leader is too overbearing or controlling the team will shut down and underact. If the team leader is too disengaged, others on the team will power up and overact or react. Either way, the team will become ineffective and the formerly thriving culture will diminish.

Great teams require great attention and vigilance. Like tending to a fine racing car, the wise teaming leader will pay close attention to the hum of the engines, to the fine-tuning efforts that keep all of the people (that is, parts) interconnected, well-adjusted, and fueled for the journey.

The one characteristic that tends to set great teaming leaders apart from just good or mediocre ones is vigilance. Great teaming leaders stay vigilant. They are tuned in to the team, the people on the team, and the synergy coming from the team. They watch for the good, and sometimes great, accomplishments, and they celebrate them. Also, they look for challenges or struggles and they bring attention to them, not to criticize but to analyze. There is a difference. Criticism can discourage a team; analysis can further challenge the team to greatness.

In this final chapter, we take a look at the indicators of a failing team culture and a thriving one. We look at team trouble signs and team vital signs. We also consider the characteristics of the mind that thinks like a teaming leader, or what I call circle thinking.

Team Trouble Signs— Diminishing Team Culture

How can you tell if your team is falling behind, faltering, or failing? Here is a list of indicators that something (or someone) in your team needs your attention or assistance. Any one or more of these troubles left unattended can quickly shut down the effective flow and function of your team. Here are some of the warning signs that indicate you or your church are missing true teaming culture:

There's Lots of Team Talk but No Real Communication

It is quite easy for a team to confuse the sounds of people in the room talking with true interaction and communication. Communication is more about honesty and understanding than the amount of words spoken. Smart teams and team players care more about coming to consensus than just merely airing their opinions. While it can certainly be invigorating to express passions and preferences, communication is more about the efforts to find common ground in the context of a faith community leading to purposeful accomplishments for the kingdom of God.

The Team Meetings Are Too Formal and Too Awkward

If you don't laugh often with your team, then you may be taking yourselves (and even your team) just a little too seriously. One important factor that plays into awkward team meetings is the location in which you meet. Some church teams hold every meeting in a boardroom. I would contend that doing so would be like having to eat every meal during the week at home in a formal dining room. Who wants to do that? Not me. That's way too formal for everyday life. Location impacts atmosphere, and atmosphere affects people's level of comfort. Find a warm and engaging location for your team meetings. And, switching out for a new location periodically is also a good idea. One pastor, Barden Gerace, always has a meal brought in for his board before every board meeting. Not only does it provide a convenience to the board members as they take another night out of their week, that is a smart thing to do as a teaming leader. Sharing a meal is also a great way to break the formalities and build the sense of team togetherness.

The Same People Always Dominate the Team Discussions

This is an age-old problem with boards, small groups, and committees. Temperaments are, of course, a big factor in who will or will not tend to carry, or even monopolize, the conversations. Wise team leaders will periodically walk their team through temperament surveys (that is, MBTI, Smalley-Trent, DISC, and so on) to help the team and team members develop healthy self-awareness. True teaming leaders also work hard at facilitating discussion techniques that draw in the entire team. It is a huge mistake to allow the people who never talk to never talk. Another approach for the team leader/facilitator is to not only ask questions of the entire team but also to periodically ask them of specific team members. (that is, "Jeff, we haven't heard from you yet today. What do you think about this question?")

There Is So Much Sarcasm That Sincerity Is Scarce

Sarcasm may be at an all-time high today with all of the talk shows, podcasts, comedy channels, YouTube clips, and social media resources. It seems that sarcasm has become a sport and a new art form. It can sometimes become quite difficult to determine which contributions of team members are sincere and genuine. The wise teaming leader will watch the amount of sarcasm happening on their team and endeavor to find ways to affirm the sincere contributions and comments of their fellow team members. Paul told Timothy, "I have been reminded of your sincere faith" (2 Tim 1:5 NIV).

The Team Members Cannot Easily Describe the Team Goals

Vision leaks. Have you noticed? One reason communicating—and recommunicating—the team's vision and goals is so important is that they can tend to quickly fade in our minds if not emphasized repeatedly. The only way to stay on the same page as a team is to write that page together and find ways to stay on it and rehearse it as well. Great teams know their goals so well, they not only can say them, but they can also see them.

The Team Interacts but Fails to Act

Never mistake interaction with action. While healthy interaction and communication helps teams determine priorities and goals, simply talking about them will not bring them to pass. Action begins once the hopes and ideas turn to plans, tasks, goals, deadlines, and accomplishments. Every great team is not just an interaction team, but an action team.

The Leader Calls It a Team but Makes the Decisions

Teams are so popular today as an approach to leadership that some churches have teams that are teams in name only. The hierarchical leader can call his team "team" a thousand times over, but if he doesn't treat the team in a teaming manner—no one is fooled by the semantics. One of the most motivating privileges of being on a team is being able to be a part of the decision-making process. When the leader makes all the decisions, the team members wonder why they are needed.

Team Members Are Guarded

Some people are intimidated by staff meetings, for the concern that they might say something wrong, stupid, or detrimental to their ministry position or jobs. This is usually an indication of some level of fear in the culture. This kind of self-protection and oversensitivity usually comes because of low (or no) trust.

People Are Confused about Their Roles

There are frequent uncertainties about who is responsible for what on the team. Little time is taken to discuss the roles and responsibilities of each team member and how they interact.

The Team Members Are All Too Much Alike

In this case the team members have so much in common, they don't adequately challenge and stretch one another's thinking and abilities. Although everyone may seem to get along, they cannot seem to get ahead.

The Team Has a Hard Time Connecting with the Other Teams in the Church

Even though the team itself may connect and collaborate somewhat, that skill seems to stop as soon as they leave their circle. Not only do they not connect or conspire with other teams in the church, there also may be some disdain or looking down on some of those other teams, as well. This issue affects church unity.

The Team Members Never Evaluate Their Teaming Skills

Although the team may take time to evaluate sermons, services, programs, and the like, they seldom, if ever, evaluate themselves as a team. More specifically, they do not critique their function or stretch themselves to improve their collaborative skills.

Elephants in the Room Are Regularly Ignored

When unresolved conflicts emerge in the team environment, they are intentionally overlooked and disregarded. The more this is done, however, the more these negative influences and motivation drainers grow and emerge, sapping the life right out of the team.

Team Vital Signs—
Thriving Team Culture

Just as there are negative characteristics that need attention and in some cases, correction, there are also signs of a strong team. Here are some of the vital signs of a team that is coming together, working together, and growing together to get the work of ministry accomplished. These are the evidences of a team coming into a good pace and finding its stride. As your groups turn into teams and teaming cultures, these are the characteristics that will evidence the change:

Meetings Are Engaging and Interesting

People enjoy team meetings rather than dread them. They are full of engaging questions, interactions, experiences, planning, and measurements of development. Because of the community and the mile markers of accomplishments on the team, it would be difficult to be bored. Who knows, maybe a pizza or two will show up at the meeting one day, or even milkshakes! But, never boredom.

Issues Are Aired Openly and Freely

Candor is a key characteristic of a healthy team. Team members do not have to mince words, but can easily and consistently make their case and offer their challenging words. In a teaming culture, truth is valued.

Intentional Efforts Are Made to
Engage Real Communication

The teaming leader frequently uses provoking questions, revealing surveys and inventories, and small group discussions to further enhance full communication on the team. From subjects that are lighter and more familiar to those that tap the deeper places in people's lives and souls, true teams and teaming cultures are interactive.

Everyone Is a Part of the Team Discussions

Much more important than the vote they represent on the team is the way team members engage their opportunities to discuss and contribute. Smart teaming leaders find ways to bring everyone in on the conversation. Certainly every team will have a few members who are naturally more fluent and engaged in conversations, but teaming leadership is all about bringing everyone in on the conversation. One technique for doing so is FreeWriting. In this scenario, the team leader poses the question of the moment to the team and asks them to take ten minutes to respond to the question in a journal or on a piece of paper. After the ten minutes is up, have everyone exchange their journal with a fellow team member, read what they have written, and then respond to it in writing by agreeing, disagreeing, asking clarifying questions, and so on. After this exercise, you will be surprised how many quiet team members have something to contribute and say.

Honor and Encouragement Is on the Main Menu and Sarcasm Is Only a Periodic Spice

When teaming culture is in full swing, honor and encouragements flow without promptings. This occurs for one primary reason: it has become a part of the culture of the team and the character of the team members. At this point, honor is not just something you say or do; it is someone you are. Does that mean sarcasm never shows up on a great team? No. But, instead of being the main course of conversation, it is a periodic and humorous seasoning spice!

The Team Members Can Quickly and Easily Describe the Team's Goals

In true teaming cultures, goals are constantly clarified and reclarified. Great teams visit and revisit their goals. They measure their progress toward them. They celebrate and rejoice each time they can check off a goal reached or exceeded.

The Team Is an Action Team

Great teams know how to turn ideas into action and accomplishment. They are suspicious of mere blue-sky session brainstorms. They know that dreaming is important but accomplishing is even more important. "A sluggard craves and gets nothing, / but the desires of the diligent are fully satisfied" (Prov 13:4 NIV).

The Leader Facilitates the Team in Making the Decisions

As team leaders grow in their role and the team in its depth and productivity, the roles emerge and develop. The leader becomes more of a facilitator. Instead of drawing upon his or her own leadership instincts alone, the leader finds ways to tap the insights, instincts, intuition, and resolve of the team itself.

The Team Is Uninhibited Because of the Strong Sense of Trust

One of the greatest joys of being a part of a team that has hit its stride is the freedom that individual team members feel to express their ideas, concerns, and hopes. Since such a teaming environment is focused on bringing out the best in the team, team members are urged to be honest and straightforward.

The Team Members Are Varied and Colorful in Personality, Strengths, and Style

Variety is the spice of life! And, there are few things more boring than being on a committee or group in which everyone is the same. A great team is a colorful team filled with confident individuals who have learned how to live and work interdependently.

People Clear about Their Roles

While great teams and teaming cultures invite cross pollination, collaboration, and partnership, they also practice clarity in roles and responsibilities. One of the ways the team stays focused is by understanding the part that each team member plays and keeping on that part. Whenever a team player drifts into another member's responsibility or a duplicated one, mutual accountability comes into play. "Wait a minute. That is my responsibility, right?"

The Team Engages Strong Teaming Skills Inside Their Own Team and With Other Teams

True teaming cultures work not only within each individual team but also among teams. A great teaming church requires more than just the pastoral staff working as a team. It means that the deacon, elders, youth staff, children's ministry, ushers, women's ministry, and so on, all function as true teams. But, it also means that the various teams find ways to collaborate and team together on projects. True teaming culture is 360 degrees!

The Team Frequently Evaluates Their Teaming Skills

Here are some evaluation questions regularly asked by teams determined to improve their teaming skills: How are we doing at this team thing? Are we as collaborative as we could be? How can we tell? What was the most effective team decision we have ever made? What made it so good? What are some things that would improve our team meetings? What would sharpen our discussions and decisions as a team?

Elephants in the Room Are Scoped Out and Annihilated

With apologies to animal lovers, the sharper the team becomes the more of a sharpshooter it becomes with elephants in the room! They are simply not tolerated no matter how many times they try to show up.

Circle Thinking

Leading a teaming church consistently and effectively involves more than teambuilding; it requires culture making. It will also involve not just building a team, but building teams of teaming leaders.

While teambuilding requires using new practices and techniques, creating a team culture requires new thinking and helping your team members think in new ways as well. I call it "circle thinking," because in lieu of thinking in a linear fashion and working on lists and tasks, the teaming leader thinks in circular dimensions. In other words, they think in ways that draw people together in smaller dynamic units of worship, relationship, and service. Here are a few essential disciplines of circle thinking:

Circle Thinking Draws Upon the Wisdom of the Team

Just as Paul used the metaphor of the church as a body in his efforts to unify the disconnected Corinthian church, so the teaming leader draws upon the resources of that body. He or she realizes that the body of Christ collectively possesses the "mind of Christ." This could also be looked at as *the team mind*, for Scripture says, "we have the mind of Christ" (1 Cor 2:16). Notice Paul didn't say, "I have the mind of Christ."

Circle Thinking Considers Not Only the Immediate Impact of Decisions but also the Ultimate Impact

The wisdom of teams is seen in the resources of foresight and projection. The difference between the solo thinker and team thinking is akin to that of checkers versus chess. Teams and their collective thinking don't just consider an organization's next moves, but what additional steps they may lead to. These are the team steps.

Circle Thinking Doesn't Just Consider What Will Take Us Further, But Also What Will Bring Us Together

At a time when church growth continues to be so many leaders' primary focus, we rarely hear about the priority of unity in the church, except, of course, in the high priestly prayer of Jesus in John 17. Wise team leadership gives consideration to team health as well as church growth. The teaming leader, or pastor, places great value on the priority of unity.

Circle Thinking Understands That If You Change One Thing, It Has an Effect on Everything

Teaming leaders and thinkers think more systemically than systematically. In other words, they consider the church as an organism, as something organic, something living, not machinelike. Because of this view, they realize that when they change one thing within the church, in a sense it changes everything. So, when changes are made they consider what else needs to change so the body can continue to grow. They pay prayerful and watchful attention to team systems.

Circle Thinking Means Considering How the Team Can Reflect the Nature of the Trinity

Teaming leaders in the church know that ultimately teams are brought together to help get the work of the kingdom of God accomplished. However, they also realize that what we do for God is important, but the way we do it is either equally or more important. The will of God and the ways of God are always on their minds. Every team is not just a task agent but another opportunity to reflect the nature of God, the Divine Team.

Circle Thinking Means Community

Teaming leaders in the church know that ultimately teams are brought together not only to accomplish tasks but also to do so together. God is a community of persons and we are called into community. And experiencing community means a growth in intimacy—intimacy with God and with others.

Rod Cooper has a great definition for the word "intimacy." He spells it this way: INTO-ME-SEE! When all of our projects and ministry jobs are said and done, what will remain are the relationships that have formed with God, with one another, and together with God. Community, teams, and teaming leadership provide the best way to move beyond ourselves, our selfishness, and to get into God's presence.

The teaming church can bring us into meaningful relationship with the people of God and into meaningful service to a world full of needs, needs that can best be met by Jesus Christ and the teaming leaders committed to his service. The teaming church will thrive as followers of Christ serve amidst circles of honor and find ways to draw new circles into which people can come, commune, and learn how to draw circles themselves.

A Teaming Leader Interview, Veteran: Tommy Barnett

Tommy Barnett, lead pastor, Phoenix First Assembly, Arizona, founder of The Dream Centers (Los Angeles and New York City), www.phoenixfirst.org, www.dreamcenter.org

One of the most prolific ministry team builders in the past fifty years has been Pastor Tommy Barnett of Phoenix, Arizona. There is no person I know who is more effective at bringing people together to accomplish good things for God's glory than Tommy.

Tommy has drawn circles all over the world in which people can dream, serve, and thrive. He is a consummate team builder and a constant honor giver.

A few years ago I had the opportunity to visit Tommy and his son, Matthew, at the Dream Center in Los Angeles. They took me on a tour of a behemoth facility that houses more than one hundred different ministries to people in the inner city. One of my great thrills was preaching in the historic Angeles Temple, the house of worship that was built by the early Pentecostal pioneer Aimee Semple McPherson.

True to form, Tommy made sure that sometime during our time together—in this case it was over pizza following the service—that he took a moment to look me in the eyes and to affirm something he saw. "Robert, you are an innovator; you're innovative." That's what true teaming leaders do.

Pastor of Phoenix First Assembly and founder of the Dream Center in Los Angeles, Tommy has proven that the teaming church model is reproducible and lasting. Phoenix First has eighteen thousand congregants and more than one hundred Dream Centers around the world.

Q: What do you know about teams and teaming leadership today that you did not know twenty-five years ago?

A: Continually cast vision. I have learned over the years the importance of sharing vision on a regular basis. You can't rely on one moment of inspiration to keep your leaders and teams motivated to do great things. It is important to meet with your leaders on a regular basis and continually share the vision, encourage them to run with the vision, and then trust them with it.

Q: What role would you say ministry teams have played in the growth of Phoenix First and the Dream Centers?

A: I may be the one leading with the vision and dream but my leadership can only accomplish things in relation to what the team is able and willing to do. Over the years I have spent time and energy casting vision while keeping proper focus on where God would lead the church and me. The result of doing this has led to spectacular growth at Phoenix First and the miracle known as the Dream Center. God did it but it took a team of people to step out and believe that it could actually happen. It takes God's dream becoming my dream and then my dream must find its way into my leaders' hearts. Then, and only then, can a dream become a reality.

Q: What makes for a great ministry team? What characterizes them?

A: Unity is the key characteristic of a strong team. When a group of people share the same goals, vision, and purposes, you can rest assured that this team will be effective in ministry.

Q: How important is a great goal to a great team?

A: A great goal is a goal that is well-defined. The more specifics you can give a ministry team, the more comfortable they will be in organizing themselves for the assignment. Great teams rally around what they understand.

Q: What are one or two of the goals at Phoenix First and the Dream Centers that you have seen motivate teams the most?

A: Each year we enter into the fall with what we call "The Season of Compassion." This is a time that we as a church capitalize on the holidays that close out a year. It begins with October 31, "Trunk or Treat," Thanksgiving's "The Great Turkey Give Away," and winds down with the Christmas double whammy, "Celebration of Christmas Musical" and "The Toy and Bike Giveaway." This is a monumental undertaking. Each event requires many teams of volunteers to make it happen. Financially it is very demanding and the vast amount time it takes to make this season a success is hard to measure. Every year we meet our goal of reaching the community with our "Big Days." Even though the events aren't easy, and the goals aren't small, out of all this we see teams created, established, and motivated to do great things for the kingdom of God.

Q: What characterizes the most effective team members at Phoenix First? What does it take to be a great team player?

A: The process of elevating people into leadership creates the opportunity for you to see a person in action. This allows you to get a feel for the quality of leadership they will provide. An effective team member is in it to help the team not help themselves.

Q: Have the ingredients of a great ministry team at Phoenix First changed as the church has grown? In other words, do the things that constitute a great team in a megachurch differ at all from those that constitute a great team in a small- or medium-sized church? Explain.

A: The ingredients of a great ministry team for churches of all sizes are the same. Set goals, dream big, and work hard to accomplish it. This is especially true when you are dealing with the condition of the human soul. You see, it doesn't matter whether you are ministering to one or one thousand, it is still ministry. It is a huge mistake to segment church leadership needs according to the size of membership. The responsibilities of a ministry team are the same—expand the kingdom of God. Great teams and great leaders are always dreaming big, setting big goals, and getting them accomplished.

Q: What does it take to build a great team?

A: Creating an atmosphere of success by casting a big vision is a must. People have to feel like they are part of something special and that the dream will not happen unless they are included. Great teams are built when a leader continually keeps the vision and dream before the people.

Q: What makes for a great team meeting? What tends to motivate and inspire people the most in team meetings?

A: Be prepared! You have to do more than just set aside time for a meeting, you have to be prepared for the meeting and take advantage of the time you have with your leaders. I have come to know that people are motivated when as a leader I set expectations and create accountability with them. When I, ahead of time, think through what I need to convey to the team I am more at ease and as a result I give the attention to my leaders that they deserve. This is inspiring to everyone involved.

Q: What makes for a poor team meeting? What tends to drain people in meetings?

A: Time is of the essence. Meetings that start late or end late usually end up making people feel like time has been wasted. People are less drained after a meeting when it has started and ended on time. They are much happier going to a meeting and will participate more fully when they know their time is respected and will, in turn, accomplish what they came to do.

Q: What undermines teams and their effectiveness? What are some typical problems that hinder the effectiveness of ministry teams?

A: When people are self-motivated and not selflessly motivated, then you can be sure that the efforts of the team will be undermined. Even the strongest leader will have to deal with ego and he must make a lasting decision not to take the spotlight and make efforts to place it on others. A glory hog or a person who somehow has found the word "me" in team can be frustrating and hinder effective ministry.

Q: What are some essentials for being a great team leader?

A: There are many things you need to look for when seeking out a great team leader. Here are just a few important habits and traits that point to strong leadership.

1. The strong leader develops a set of goals with all their team members.

2. The strong leader doesn't dwell on problems, but concentrates energies on solutions.

3. The strong leader will constantly remind the team of the goals and plans.

4. The strong leader develops team spirit among the members and volunteers.

Drawing Your Circle

Questions to Ask Your Team

1. What are some ways to refresh your team or team members?

2. What would make your team meetings more engaging and interesting?

3. What are two ways that communication and discussions could be improved on your team?

4. Is your team more of an action team or a discussion group?

5. How are decisions generally made on your team? Is it a team process? Is it as prompt and precise a process as it could be? What would improve this?

6. How long do elephants get to live in your team meetings?

7. Do your team, team leader, and team members practice circle thinking? Explain.

Once Upon
a Team—
Final Scene

The Final Cup

"Everything alright?" Glenn asked, taking his seat again at the small table.

"Yes, everything is fine," Scott said.

"Are you sure?"

"Well, if I am going to exercise real candor as you suggested earlier . . . NO. Apparently, I somehow forgot I was supposed to take my mother-in-law's car to a mechanic shop this morning. Oops!"

"Do you need to leave now?"

"No. I was supposed to pick her car up a half-hour ago and it just slipped my mind. But I am pretty sure I know why it did."

"Senior moment?"

"No, I'm thirty-five, so I can't use that excuse. No, it was something else."

"What's that?"

"A great talk with a good new friend."

"Glad you feel that way, Scott. I count it a privilege."

"And an honor, right?" Scott added with a smile.

"How could I forget that great word. That's a fact. So, you don't need to scoot and take care of your mother-in-law?"

"No, since I missed it, my wife rescheduled it for this afternoon. I will take care of it then, so that gives us a few more minutes to talk."

"Well, I must say I sort of envy you, Scott."

"How so? Because I get to take my mother-in-law's car to the shop?"

"No, because you are still a young man with decades ahead of you to serve the kingdom of God and build great people and great teams!"

"I hope I can learn to do so and improve at it. Honestly, I think I have a lot yet to learn."

"Join the club. Life's a never-ending university. You just have to stay interested, open-minded, and at the task. It's a new world, Scott. In some ways because of technology we are more connected than ever before, but I find that most people have become quite disconnected emotionally, ironically so."

"I sense that. That's really true."

"So then, you and your church have a great opportunity to be an environment that not only builds great teams but also a great community. One so great that you not only work and worship together but you also reflect something of the very nature and glory of God as you do so."

"That sounds like a great goal. Almost unattainable."

"Downright impossible from a human level, if you ask me," Glenn said. "But it will take a great goal or great conflict to stretch you and to stretch your church. And, my experience has been as a pastor that if you and your church are not reaching and stretching toward a great goal, you're stuck; you're dead in the water."

"Hmm," Scott said. Glenn could see the tumblers falling into place for his new friend. "Wow, this time has been so helpful, Glenn. I really appreciate you meeting with me. It is going to take me about a week to unpack all of these insights we have discussed. Really great stuff."

"Well, one week is just about right," Glenn said, "because I was going to suggest we meet again for coffee next week, same time, same place. How's that sound?"

"Sounds like a plan."

Glenn and Scott shook hands and departed.

As Glenn drove back home, he whispered a prayer: "Lord, thank you for a new friend and for a new place to invest some of the things others have invested in me."

As Scott drove off, he felt excited about the new mentor and friend he had found and a new sense of anticipation and hope about the future of the church he served, the challenges he faced, and the teams he was determined to build. As he thought more about what this meeting had meant to him and why the time had gone by so fast talking with Glenn, the word suddenly came to mind that perfectly described the way he felt . . .

Honored.

NOTES

INTRODUCTION: THE CIRCLES JESUS DREW

1. Gilbert Bilezikian, *Community 101* (Grand Rapids: Zondervan, 1997), 11–12.

1. THE DAY YOUR GROUP BECOMES A TEAM

1. Trey Thoelcke, ed., *Building Effective Teams* (Chicago: Dearborn Trade Publishing, 2005), 1.

2. Adapted from a definition of teams included in Jon R. Katzenback and Douglas K. Smith, *The Wisdom of Teams* (New York: HarperBusiness, 2003), 45.

3. Desmond Tutu, *No Future without Forgiveness* (New York: Doubleday, 1999), 31.

2. THE TEAM TOUR: GREAT TEAMS AND TEAMING PLAYERS

1. "Life Together," *Christianity Today* 45, no. 9 (July 9, 2001): 26.

2. Ibid.

3. J. Peterson, "Labor Department Panel Urges Teaching New Skills for Jobs," *Los Angeles Times* (July 3, 1991): D-1.

4. Frank LaFasto and Carl Larson, *When Teams Work Best: 6000 Team Members and Leaders Tell What It Takes to Succeed* (Thousand Oaks, Calif.: Sage Publications, 2001), xvii.

5. Ibid.

6. Mattison Crowe, "Why the Members of Your Team Won't Speak Up, and What You Can Do About It," *Teams That Click* (Boston: Harvard Business School Press, 2004), 93–94.

7. Jon R. Katzenbach and Douglas K. Smith, *The Wisdom of Teams*, 2nd ed. (New York: HarperCollins, 2003).

8. From the foreword by Ken Blanchard in Laurie Beth Jones, *Teach Your Team to Fish* (New York: Three Rivers Press, 2002), xi

9. Katzenbach and Smith, *The Wisdom of Teams*, 11.

10. Ibid., xiii.

11. Ibid., xix.

12. Patrick Lencioni, *Overcoming the Five Dysfunctions of a Team: A Field Guide* (San Francisco: Jossey-Bass, 2005), 3.

13. It is reasonable to also conclude that one reason the early church used teams so effectively was because of the great goal (that is, Great Commission of Christ) that it lived with daily. The Holy Spirit at work in the church was determined to reach Jerusalem, Judea, Samaria and "the uttermost part of the earth" (Acts 1:8 ASV). The method of choice to carry out the great task was dynamic and fast-moving ministry teams, or teams.

14. Robert Simons, "Designing High Performance Jobs," *Harvard Business Review* (July–August 2005): 58.

15. Katzenbach and Smith, *The Wisdom of Teams,* xiv., 3.

16. Amy Edmondson, "Teamwork on the Fly: How to Master the New Art of Teaming," *Harvard Business Review* (April 2012): 74.

17. Katzenbach and Smith, xxiv.

18. A better biblical term to use in place of "smarter" would be "wiser." Consider the passage, "If you want to win, you need many good advisers" (Prov 24:6b NIrV).

19. James Surowiecki, *The Wisdom of Crowds: Why the Many Are Smarter than the Few and How Collective Wisdom Shapes Business, Economies, Societies and Nations* (New York: Doubleday, 2004), 222.

20. Ibid., 207–8.

21. Jack Welch, *Winning* (New York: HarperCollins, 2005), 29–30.

22. Alex Pentland, "The New Science of Building Great Teams," *Harvard Business Review* (April 2012): 66.

23. Ibid, 62.

24. Ken Blanchard, Donald Carew, and Eunice Parisi-Carew, *The One Minute Manager Builds High Performing Teams* (New York: Morrow, 2000), vii.

25. Robert Simons, "Designing High Performance Jobs," *Harvard Business Review* (July–August 2005): 58.

26. Erwin Raphael McManus, *An Unstoppable Force: Daring to Become the Church God Had in Mind* (Loveland, Colo.: Group Books, 2001), 14.

27. Peter F. Drucker, "Drucker on Management: There's More Than One Kind of Team," *Wall Street Journal* (Feb. 11, 1992), http://online.wsj.com/article/SB100 0142405274870420430457544312916277426.html.

28. Bill Hybels, *Courageous Leadership* (Grand Rapids: Zondervan, 2002), 75.

3. THE DNA OF A WINNING TEAM

1. From the foreword by Rick Warren in Erwin Raphael McManus, *An Unstoppable Force: Daring to Become the Church God Had in Mind* (Loveland, Colo.: Group Books, 2001), 6.

2. Randolph Bourne, "The Excitement of Friendship," *The Atlantic Monthly* (December 1912), http://www.monadnock.net/bourne/friendship.html.

3. John Kotter, Leading Change (Boston: Harvard Business School Press, 1996), 61.

4. Patrick Lencioni, *Overcoming the Five Dysfunctions of a Team: A Field Guide* (San Francisco: Jossey-Bass, 2005), 14, 18.

5. Alex Pentland, "The New Science of Building Great Teams," *Harvard Business Review* (April 2012): 62.

6. Ibid., 65.

5. TURNING GROUPS INTO TEAMS

1. John Maxwell, *Leadership Gold* (Nashville: Thomas Nelson, 2008), 66 (italics mine).

2. Arthur C. Smith, *Team and Group Ministry* (Westminster, UK: Church Information Office, 1965), 9.

3. Peter Croft, *The Team Ministry* (Westminster, UK: Church of England, Church Information Office, 1966), 4.

4. Smith, 9.

5. Ibid., 86.

6. Bruce Tuckman, "Developmental Sequence in Small Groups," *Psychological Bulletin* 63, no. 6 (1965): 384–99.

6. TEAMING LEADERSHIP

1. John Wesley's letter to Alexander Mather on August 6, 1777 (*Letters*, 6:272).

2. Stephen A. Macchia, *Becoming a Healthy Team: Five Traits of Vital Leadership* (Grand Rapids: Baker Books, 2005), 17.

3. Leonard Sweet, *Aqua Church: Essential Leadership Arts for Piloting Your Church in Today's Fluid Culture* (Loveland, Colo.: Group Publishing, 1999), 188.

4. James M. Kouzes and Barry Z. Posner, *The Leadership Challenge* (San Francisco: Jossey-Bass, 1987), 135.

5. Alex Pentland, "The New Science of Building Great Teams," *Harvard Business Review* (April 2012): 70.

6. Ibid.

7. Sweet, *Aqua Church*, 188.

7. ESSENTIAL SKILLS OF TEAMING LEADERS: UNLEASHING TEAM BRILLIANCE

1. Leonard Sweet, *Aqua Church: Essential Leadership Arts for Piloting Your Church in Today's Fluid Culture* (Loveland, Colo.: Group Publishing, 1999), 347.

2. Jon R. Katzenbach and Douglas K. Smith, *The Wisdom of Teams*, 2nd ed. (New York: HarperCollins Publishers, 2003), xvii.

3. Amy Edmondson, "Teamwork on the Fly: How to Master the New Art of Teaming," *Harvard Business Review* (April 2012): 74.

4. *Conversation Starters for Couples* and *Conversation Starters for Parents and Kids* (Colorado Springs, Colo.: Focus on the Family, 2006).

5. Amy Edmondson, "Teamwork on the Fly: How to Master the New Art of Teaming," *Harvard Business Review* (June 2012), 79.

6. Michael Marquardt, *Leading with Questions: How Leaders Find the Right Solutions by Knowing What to Ask* (San Francisco: Jossey-Bass, 2005), 23–24.

7. Ibid.

8. Jim Kling, "Tension in Teams," *Harvard Business Review* (Jan. 14, 2009), http://blogs.hbr.org/hmu/2009/01/tension-in-teams.html.

9. As cited in Craig E. Runde and Tim A. Flanagan, *Building Conflict Competent Teams* (San Francisco: Jossey-Bass, 2008), 119.

8. THE DIVINE TEAM

1. Stanley J. Grenz, *Rediscovering the Triune God: The Trinity in Contemporary Theology* (Minneapolis: Fortress, 2004), 1.

2. Stanley J. Grenz, *The Social God and the Relational Self: A Trinitarian Theology of the Imago Dei* (London: Westminster John Knox, 2001), 55 (italics mine).

3. Andy Stanley and Bill Willits, *Creating Community: Five Keys to Building a Small Group Culture* (Sisters, Ore.: Multnomah, 2004), 41.

4. Stanley J. Grenz, *Theology for the Community of God* (Grand Rapids: Eerdmans, 2000), 484.

5. E. Stanley Ott, *Transform Your Church with Ministry Teams* (Grand Rapids: Eerdmans, 2004), 5.

6. Grenz, *Theology for the Community of God*, 101–2.

7. George Cladis, *Leading the Team-Based Church* (San Francisco: Jossey-Bass, 1999), 4-5.

8. Amy Planting Pauw, *The Supreme Harmony of All: The Trinitarian Theology of Jonathan Edwards* (Grand Rapids: Eerdmans, 2002).

9. Grenz, *Theology for the Community of God*, 71.

10. Dallas Willard, *The Divine Conspiracy* (San Fransisco: Harper San Francisco, 1998), 318.

11. John B. Champion, *Personality and the Trinity* (London: Fleming H. Revell Co., 1935), 103.

12. Gilbert Bilezikian, *Community 101* (Grand Rapids: Zondervan, 1997), 27.

9. TEAMING MODELS AND METAPHORS: THE IMAGES THAT HELP US DRAW BETTER CIRCLES

1. Andy Crouch, "Visualcy: Literacy Is Not the Only Necessity in a Visual Culture," *Christianity Today* (May 31, 2005), http://www.christianitytoday.com/ct/2005/june/21.62.html.

2. Howard A. Snyder, *Models of the Kingdom* (Nashville: Abingdon Press, 1991), 15.

3. Lawrence O. Richards, *Expository Dictionary of Bible Words* (Grand Rapids: Zondervan, 1985), 262.

4. Gilbert Bilezikian, *Community 101* (Grand Rapids: Zondervan, 1997), 54.

5. Bill Hybels, *Courageous Leadership* (Grand Rapids: Zondervan, 2002), 75.

6. Leonard Sweet, *Aqua Church: Essential Leadership Arts for Piloting Your Church in Today's Fluid Culture* (Loveland, Colo.: Group Publishing, 1999), 191.

Robert C. Crosby is a communicator, ministry leader, and author. He and his wife, Pamela, have pastored for more than twenty-five years, in New York, Ohio, and Boston. He has served as a vice president at Southeastern University and currently is training a new generation of young ministers there as professor of practical theology.

Crosby has written several books including *More Than a Savior,* which was recently released as a Kindle and Nook e-book. He has a blog and column at Patheos.com and is a contributing writer to *Christianity Today, Leadership Journal,* and the *Pentecostal Evangel.*

He and his wife, Pamela, have four children: Kristin, Kara, Rob, and Kandace. Together they have written two books for Focus on the Family *Conversation Starters for Couples* and *Conversation Starters for Parents and Kids.* They also minister to families through Better Together, a conference and resource ministry to churches, families, and leaders. He and Pamela speak at marriage conferences throughout the country.

To schedule Robert Crosby for a speaking engagement, conference, Teaming Church Conference, church consultation, leadership or couples events, contact: Better Together Resources and Conferences at rccrosby@aol.com.

> **"One of the most important tools for any team leader is great questions. The wise leader of teams today uses questions to challenge and inspire his team to greatness."**
>
> *—Robert Crosby*

Download the New Mobile App from Robert Crosby & GloBible

Great Questions to Ask Your Team, Your Spouse & Your Kids!

For a free set of great team questions and to get more information on the "Ask Up!" app, go to:

www.globible.com/AskUp/

Or use the QR Code: